COLLECTOR'S VALUE GUIDE™

Cherished Teddies®

Secondary Market Price Guide & Collector Handbook

THIRD EDITION

This publication is *not* affiliated with Enesco Corporation or any of its affiliates, subsidiaries, distributors or representatives. Any opinions expressed are solely those of the authors, and do not necessarily reflect those of Enesco Corporation. **"Cherished Teddies®"** is a registered trademark of Enesco Corporation. Product names and product designs are the property of Enesco Corporation. Artwork used with permission.

All secondary market pricing is compiled through an independent sampling of retailers, collectors and secondary market dealers. The Enesco Corporation is not involved in any way in the establishment of secondary market prices. The registration number on the understamp of each figurine should be used as a general guideline to the year that individual piece was manufactured (i.e., 559/852 = 1995). Each registration number is hand-numbered, however, and on occasion errors may be made and a number other than the year of production may be used.

Front cover: "Winfield" (Special Millennium Limited Edition)
Back cover (left to right): "Teddy and Roosevelt" (LE-1993), "Cherished Teddies Town Sign" (1995 Event Exclusive), "Priscilla Ann" (1994-95 Expo Exclusive)

Managing Editor:	Jeff Mahony	Art Director:	Joe T. Nguyen
Associate Editors:	Melissa A. Bennett	Production Supervisor:	Scott Sierakowski
	Jan Cronan	Senior Graphic Designers:	Carole Mattia-Slater
	Gia C. Manalio		Leanne Peters
	Paula Stuckart	Graphic Designers:	Jennifer J. Denis
Contributing Editor:	Mike Micciulla		Lance Doyle
Editorial Assistants:	Jennifer Filipek		Sean-Ryan Dudley
	Nicole LeGard Lenderking		Kimberly Eastman
	Christina Levere		Ryan Falis
	Joan C. Wheal		Jason C. Jasch
Research Assistants:	Timothy R. Affleck		David S. Maloney
	Priscilla Berthiaume		David Ten Eyck
	Heather N. Carreiro	Art Intern:	Janice Evert
	Beth Hackett		
	Victoria Puorro		
	Steven Shinkaruk		
Web Reporters:	Samantha Bouffard		
	Ren Messina		

ISBN 1-888914-51-3

(formerly Collectors' Publishing)
306 Industrial Park Road • Middletown, CT 06457

TABLE OF CONTENTS

TABLE OF CONTENTS

Introducing The Collector's Value Guide™

*C*ongratulations! You are holding in your hands the Third Edition of the **Collector's Value Guide™ to Cherished Teddies®**. Flip through the pages to discover an easy-to-use, reliable and informative resource for this charming line of collectibles from artist Priscilla Hillman.

An Inside Look

Cherished Teddies figurines are a collection of warm memories and innocence and what better way to share in these memories than to see them through the eyes of their creator. In our exclusive interview, Priscilla Hillman talks about her work and life in a way that will inform and delight you. After the interview, check out the spotlight on Hillman's other lines from Enesco – teddies aren't her only passion!

Bears O'Plenty!

And then it's off to the wonderful world of the teddies. Meet the assortment of new releases in the "What's New" section, brush up on the latest club news, say goodbye to the 1999 retirements and discover the "Top Ten," which lists the most "cherished" teddies of them all!

You Mean There's MORE?

The Value Guide offers full-color photos of the **Cherished Teddies** line along with all of the pertinent information you need to know about your favorite pieces. Next, additional **Cherished Teddies** products are spotlighted, along with gift and display ideas, secondary market information, variations and insurance information. Are you ready? Then, *let's take a look!*

CHERISHED TEDDIES® OVERVIEW

*W*hile teddy bears have long been a favorite among the young and the young-at-heart, the Enesco Corporation and artist Priscilla Hillman have taken this popularity to a new level with her **Cherished Teddies** line of adorable teddy bear figurines.

As a child, Priscilla and her twin sister spent hours at the kitchen table with water-colors and sketch pads. For Hillman, this pastime developed into a career of illustrating children's books and, eventually, providing Enesco Corporation with original art-work which is the basis for a number of popular collectible figurine lines.

"BEAR WINDOW"

While recuperating from a back injury in the late 1980s, Hillman mentally accumulated a portfolio of characters and ideas to ease the tedium of her recovery. During this period, she also surrounded herself with albums of cherished photos from her past and caught up on classic TV movie reruns. All of these nostalgic images came to life in the illustrations that Hillman submitted to Mr. Eugene Freedman of Enesco in 1991. Priscilla Hillman's "drawings in her mind" became reality when the first teddy bear figurines were introduced the following year as part of the new **Cherished Teddies** line.

Within two years of its introduction, the collection was named "Collectible of the Year" in 1993 and the ted-dies' creator was named "Artist of the Year" in 1994 by the National Association of Limited Edition Dealers (NALED). This immediate recognition in the world of collectibles established Hillman and her teddies as an overnight success, much to her amazement. From this small assortment of figurines, almost 1,000 teddies have escaped the Enesco lair.

A "TEDDIE" TO CHERISH

Similar in style to the familiar teddy bear found in many children's toy boxes, the **Cherished Teddies** design is immediately recognizable. The entire clan is replicated with neatly brushed blond fur, often with a patched or worn area on the bottom of the feet. Their faces feature a pair of expressive eyes with a classic down-turned bear mouth. Many styles of bows, ribbons and attire complete the distinctive look of the line.

This year, with the addition of over 170 new pieces to the **Cherished Teddies** collection, Enesco has provided collectors even more opportunities to select the teddie that is special to them. Figurines are the largest category in the line, but that's not all. Quite a selection of frames has been produced, as well as clocks, musicals, waterglobes, ornaments and more. For collectors of plates and plaques, many with a holiday or seasonal theme are available. The dilemma remains, however, of which ones to choose to take home with you!

TEDDIES ACROSS THE SEAS
AND AIMIN' TO PLEASE!

Collecting a den full of these diminutive darlings will expose you to Priscilla Hillman's wonderful world of teddie scenarios. She has sent her bruins around the world, dressed them up for the holidays, given them friends with whom to share secrets and provided them with a quiet demeanor of unconditional love.

CHERISHED TEDDIES® OVERVIEW

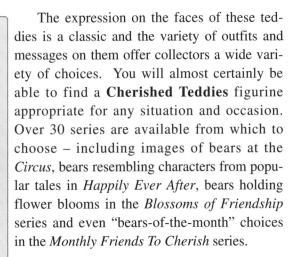

Production

Using Priscilla Hillman's color sketches, sculptors in Asia fashion clay models from which rubber molds are made. These molds are then used to create the "white body" of the figurine to which small resin attachments are glued into place. The painting of the piece is done in steps, with the master artists providing the fine details. Finally, the name, stock number and/or title is printed on, a registration number is handwritten on and pads are attached to the bottom of each piece.

Packaging

The figurines are individually wrapped in a protective material, fitted into hard foam and then placed inside a specially designed cardboard box for **Cherished Teddies** merchandise. Each piece is accompanied by a gift card, a registration postcard and a Certificate of Adoption.

Pricing

Suggested retail pricing for **Cherished Teddies** can range from less than $10 for ornaments to over $150 for multiple-piece sets or musicals.

The expression on the faces of these teddies is a classic and the variety of outfits and messages on them offer collectors a wide variety of choices. You will almost certainly be able to find a **Cherished Teddies** figurine appropriate for any situation and occasion. Over 30 series are available from which to choose – including images of bears at the *Circus*, bears resembling characters from popular tales in *Happily Ever After*, bears holding flower blooms in the *Blossoms of Friendship* series and even "bears-of-the-month" choices in the *Monthly Friends To Cherish* series.

PLEASANTLY PLUSH

And when you think of teddie bears you have to think about those cuddly plush critters from your childhood. The first **Cherished Teddies** plush pieces, "Elsa" and "Norman," were introduced in 1993, but there were only a few new plush pieces released over the next several years. That changed recently, when Enesco began to offer a plethora of new plush pals in a lovable bean bag design. From exclusive event pieces to plush series, these teddies are sure to invoke strong sentiments in anyone who sees them.

As responsible **Cherished Teddies** collectors, we are now confronted with the daunting task of loving our teddies – come to think of it, that's the easiest part!

COLLECTOR'S
VALUE GUIDE™

*I*t's easy to see that **Cherished Teddies** figurines portray the importance and existence of happiness, friendship and love in Priscilla Hillman's life. As the artist of the teddy bear figurines, she recreates these sentiments for everyone to see through her designs.

The idea for the **Cherished Teddies** line began in the late 1980s while Hillman was recovering from a back injury. To pass the time, the former illustrator of children's books drew pictures of teddy bears with endearing expressions. After her recovery, she sent the drawings to Enesco Corporation, one of the world's leading distributors of collectibles. As Hillman puts it, "Why not start at the top and work my way down?" The attempt paid off. Enesco produced resin figurines from those drawings, and in 1992 the first pieces debuted. It didn't take long for the collecting world to catch on – the **Cherished Teddies** line quickly became one of the country's best-selling collectible lines.

What sparks an idea for a **Cherished Teddies** design? Hillman says it's anything from animals she finds in her gardens, to personal memories from the past, mainly of her and twin sister Greta playing at the beach or in their aunt and uncle's attic. She also says she gets ideas at night just before falling asleep. Priscilla now passes the time tending to her gardens, shopping for antiques for her 18th century home or just spending quality time with her husband and son.

CheckerBee Publishing recently had the chance to ask Priscilla Hillman to share a little bit about what it's like to be the designer of one of the world's top collectible lines. Here's what she had to say:

CheckerBee: Your teddies were practically an "overnight success." You had won a TOBY award within one year of the line's debut. Yet, this success has hardly gone to your head. At one show in Rosemont, Illinois you quietly tried to buy one of our Value Guides before being recognized. How does it feel to realize that you are a celebrity in the world of collectibles?

Priscilla Hillman: I don't feel like a celebrity. Sometimes I have to be "pinched" to realize that this is all real. I really enjoy seeing and meeting collectors at appearances and hearing how they appreciate my work. It has really all developed from something I truly love to do!

> ***"I don't feel like a celebrity. Sometimes I have to be 'pinched' to realize that this is all real."***

CheckerBee: In seven years, you have really grown as a working artist and this is apparent in the wonderful detail of the **Cherished Teddies** pieces, as well as the introduction of your other lines from Enesco. How have your designs evolved over the years?

Hillman: The designs seem to get better and better. There are always new ideas and themes to tie into each of the lines I work on.

CheckerBee: With six collections, it must be hard coming up with all those ideas. Do you ever get "artist's block?" If so, how do you deal with it?

Hillman: I look for inspiration all around me every day. You never know when a new idea will come or what will inspire it. Some of the best ideas come when I'm doing something I enjoy, whether I'm in the garden or at an antiques or flea market.

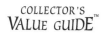

CheckerBee: Each **Cherished Teddies** character has its own distinct personality which is reflected in its outfit, activity and the accompanying phrase or title. Where do these ideas come from? Are they based on your own memories or scenes that you see while walking down the street – or a little bit of both?

Hillman: Many of my ideas are based on personal memories from childhood. And even though they are my personal memories, I think a lot of people can relate the pieces to their own lives.

CheckerBee: So what is it like to be a working artist? What does a typical workday consist of for you?

Hillman: Most days I get up early – usually around 6 o'clock in the morning. I will typically work at my desk throughout the day thinking of new ideas.

CheckerBee: After a day of work, how do you like to wind down and relax?

Hillman: I always enjoy spending time with my family. In the springtime, I like to relax outside in my English garden or play with the neighbor's cat.

CheckerBee: Family is obviously very important to you. We know that your family often accompanies you when touring and that your son and husband have recently been the inspiration behind the pieces "Glenn" and "Norm." How do they feel about being immortalized in **Cherished Teddies** figurines?

Hillman: It took some time for them to agree on what piece they wanted to "be." Each figurine was designed with themes that they could relate to. [*CheckerBee Note:* "Glenn" features a boating theme, while "Norm" features a fishing theme.]

INTERVIEW WITH PRISCILLA HILLMAN

CheckerBee: **Cherished Teddies** designs all have an antique flair to them, from their petticoats to their bonnets. I understand that this stems from your passion for nostalgia. Is this a passion that you've had since childhood?

Hillman: Yes. I have always loved nostalgic items and the Victorian era in particular.

> ### *"I've always felt it was important to preserve what we have today for the future tomorrow."*

CheckerBee: Once again your passion for the nostalgic is reflected in the New England Colonial house that you and your family live in. I imagine that you have designed it to be a place that would be a natural habitat for the teddies. Is this an accurate image?

Hillman: I have one room which is designed in particular for the teddies and I like to fill the other rooms with period antiques.

CheckerBee: You graduated from the University of Rhode Island as a botany major. With your love of the arts, it's interesting that you pursued an education in the sciences. What led you to this decision?

Hillman: I enjoyed studying the sciences because I've always been very concerned with the environment and the planet. I've always felt it was important to preserve what we have today for the future tomorrow.

CheckerBee: Among all the designs that you've created, do you have a favorite **Cherished Teddies** piece?

Hillman: I have many favorite pieces and I like them all for different reasons, but one of my all-time favorites is "Christopher," one of my early designs.

e very season brings the introduction of a bounty of wonderful new **Cherished Teddies** figurines and the 1999 spring season is no exception.

GENERAL FIGURINES

Alex . . . *Cherish The Little Things* **. . .** This adorable teddie embodies the lesson that one should always appreciate the smaller details of life like the companionship of a toy duck or the possibilities that a toy ship has to offer.

Alyssa . . . *You Warm My Soul* **. . .** Bundled up to ward off the cold, blustery breezes, this cub is dressed in her leggings, pale blue coat and matching pom-pommed hat which is pulled down over one ear. With her paws stuffed into her pockets, "Alyssa" is determined to ignore the pile of snow at her feet.

Anita . . . *You're A Tulip To Treasure* **. . .** This 1999 Catalog Exclusive welcomes spring with "Anita" dressed in her finest lavender and white pinafore and bonnet ensemble. In her apron, she carries freshly picked tulips and has her pet lamb by her side.

Anne . . . *So Glad You're Here To Keep Me Warm* **. . .** Some teddies just warm your heart and this is one of them! Her rose colored hat is slightly askew and those ear flaps aren't quite doing the job but she doesn't seem to notice!

Anxiously Awaiting The Arrival . . . Past and present "moms-to-be" will recognize the rosy glow on this lady's cheeks that comes with the joy and excitement of impending motherhood.

Arnold . . . *You "Putt" Me In A Great Mood* **. . .** Golfing can be great therapy – and it can be the best prescription for anyone feeling like a "bear." "Arnold" "putts" his best foot forward with his stylish drive!

Ava . . . *You Make Me Feel Beautiful Inside . . .* While this little lady primps herself with makeup and perfume, she knows where true beauty lies. Available for a limited time through Avon, "Ava" is sure to bring out the beauty in all who see her.

Bette . . . *You Are The Star Of The Show . . .* The 1999 Adoption Center Event Piece, "Bette" is standing on her very own "star" – on the **Cherished Teddies** Walk Of Fame, of course.

Carlin & Janay . . . *When I Count My Blessings, I Count You Twice . . .* This charming couple proves that some friends are worth DOUBLE their weight in gold and are great to have around to hug away the chill!

Charissa & Ashylynn . . . *Every Journey Begins With One Step . . .* With her Mom behind her to bolster her courage, this cub is embarking on her first trip by herself. Armed with her overnight bag and her trusty teddie, she has the ticket for her first big adventure!

Cherish . . . *Reach Out To Someone Around You . . .* This charming teddie takes her family name quite seriously and is a reminder that you should "cherish" those that surround your life.

Daisy & Chelsea . . . *Old Friends Always Find Their Way Back . . .* These two friends know that a true friendship never dies and have come back in this limited figurine to remind collectors of the power of friendship. Featuring two of the most valuable **Cherished Teddies**, this intriguing Event Exclusive will be quite a catch for collectors.

Dennis . . . *You Put The Spice In My Life . . .* When you kiss the cook, you usually get your burger the way you like it! Complete with chef hat and spatula, this Event Exclusive is ready to take your order.

Ed . . . *There's A Patch In My Heart For You . . .* This pumpkin-toting teddie has picked the best in the patch just for you! Adding this Event Piece to your collection is a must!

Fay & Arlene . . . *Thanks For Always Being By My Side . . .* This delightful rendering of sibling appreciation shows "Fay & Arlene" walking arm in arm dressed in spring frocks, pantaloons and straw hats.

Follow The Yellow Brick Road Collector Set . . . There's no place like your home for this set of beary weary travelers. "Dot," "Leo," "Scott" and "Tim"

follow their dreams and the rainbow in this special limited edition collector set.

Glenn . . . *By Land Or By Sea, Let's Go – Just You And Me . . .* This nautical navigator is ready to set sail into the collection. Named for Priscilla Hillman's son, this teddie is willing to brave the currents to sail into your family too.

Graduation . . . *Always Put Your Best Paw Forward . . .* This is indeed a smart little teddie, graduating at the top of the Avon Exclusive class. Complete with diploma in hand, this teddie knows there's no better place than your collection.

Show Exclusive!

A special **Cherished Teddies** figurine, "The Company We Keep Is A Reflection Of Ourselves," will be available only at the 1999 International Collectible Expositions in Long Beach, California (in April) and Rosemont, Illinois (in June).

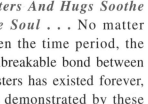

Haley and Logan . . . *Sisters And Hugs Soothe The Soul . . .* No matter when the time period, the unbreakable bond between sisters has existed forever, as demonstrated by these close siblings from an era in the past.

Hazel . . . *I've Got A Notion To Give You A Potion . . .* Witches are supposed to be frightening but poor "Hazel" couldn't scare you if she tried! Dressed in her favorite holiday colors, she is ready to sweep away the spooks at your house.

Honey . . . *You're A Good Friend That Sticks Like Honey . . .* You've never seen a more complete costume for Halloween! Dressed as a teddie bear (surprise!), this cub carries a crock of honey and a bear pull toy in one hand and his bucket of treats in another.

If A Mom's Love Comes In All Sizes, Yours Has The Biggest Of Hearts . . . What better way to say "Thanks" to mom than with this adorable piece, which is a Gift-To-Go Exclusive that will only available until Mother's Day.

Irene . . . *Time Leads Us Back To The Things We Love The Most . . .* A family's love transcends all boundaries and "Irene" knows that no matter how long she is away, her family will always be there to welcome her home with open arms.

Irish Mini Figurines . . . *Good Luck . . .* The saying goes "Good things comes in small packages," and this piece fits the bill perfectly. Only one-and-a-half inches tall, this itty bitty bear has a pot of gold and a rainbow to wish you luck.

Irish Mini Figurines . . . *Lucky Charm . . .* This charming little lass is holding your lucky horseshoe and boasts a green clover on her pullover.

Jasmine . . . *A Bouquet Of Blessings For You . . .* With a crown of fragrant blooms around her head, "Jasmine" holds a patchwork heart in this GCC Exclusive.

Jerome . . . *Can't Bear The Cold Without You . . .* This piece is guaranteed to warm you heart during the cold months of winter. As he is an Avon Exclusive, you'll have a beautiful feeling if you can add "Jerome" to your collection.

PHOTO UNAVAILABLE

Joe . . . *Love Only Gets Better With Age . . .* Over the years, "Joe" has learned that love, one of the most precious gifts in life, gets richer and stronger with age. And you'll want to grow old with this irresistible little bear as well.

John and William . . . *When Friends Meet, Hearts Warm . . .* When Christmas carols are sung on a crisp night with song sheets illuminated only by the street light, friendships are renewed and all is in tune!

Joseph . . . *Everyone Has Their "Old Friends" To Hug . . .* Surrounded by the toys of his childhood, "Joseph" brings collectors back to that time of playfulness and innocence that is often forgotten in these busy times. As part of your collection, he too will soon become an old friend.

June and Jean . . . *I've Always Wanted To Be Just Like You . . .* These twin sisters are dressed simply in bonnets of blue and pink that can be tied together to symbolize the bond they share.

Junior . . . *Everyone Is A Bear's Best Friend . . .* Holding his bunny pal in his arms, "Junior" is testimony that friendship knows no barriers and yes, we can all just get along.

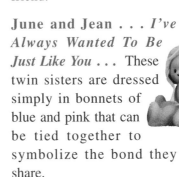

Justine and Janice . . . *Sisters and Friendship Are Crafted With Love . . .* The best of friends, these two sisters complement each other perfectly. While they may wonder what it's like to live in the other's shoes, they are happy to experience it vicariously.

Katie, Renee, Jessica, Matthew . . . *I'm Surrounded By Hugs . . .* This 1999 Event Exclusive, available in both a U.S. and International version, shows the unconditional love that a mother experiences from her brood as she's the happy recipient of a group hug!

Kayla . . . *Big Hearts Come In Small Packages . . .* Although her packages are small in size, each one is chosen by "Kayla" with care and filled with love – just as this piece was chosen as an Event Exclusive.

Kyle . . . *Even Though We're Far Apart, You'll Always Have A Place In My Heart . . .* "Kyle" testifies that indeed absence makes the heart grow fonder and that no amount of distance can cause his love to fade. However, collectors will want to keep this adorable teddie close by as a reminder of the power of love.

Loretta . . . Spring into the season with this adorable exclusive figurine. Her availability will be short but sweet . . . she'll only be around during 1999 and only at retailers who participate in syndicated catalog groups.

PHOTO UNAVAILABLE

Lori . . . *Those We Love Should Be Cherished . . .* Holding her feathered friend in her lap and resting against a giant sack of chicken feed, "Lori" demonstrates that every friend is one that we should care for.

Matt and Vicki . . . *Love Is The Best Thing Two Can Share . . .* Enjoying the cool breeze against their faces, this couple snuggles closer together as they remind us of the importance of spending time with one another.

Meredith . . . *You're As Cozy As A Pair Of Mittens!* . . . Poor "Meredith" seems to have lost her mittens! Perhaps she is hoping to find a pair to match her cozy green hat and scarf set!

Milt and Garrett . . . *A Haunting We Will Go* . . . This frightfully cute pair is ready for the annual haunting to "reap" the treats!

Mother's Day Mini Figurines . . . *Grandma* . . . Every grandma will cherish this token of love from her favorite grandchild – and we all know who her favorite is!

Mother's Day Mini Figurines . . . *Mom* . . . Every day is Mother's Day and this mini-figurine will remind her just that!

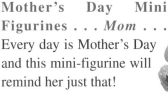

Mother's Day Mini Figurines . . . *Nana* . . . Perfect for the nana in your life, this piece shows your love that is personalized!

Natalie . . . *You Make Me Smile From Ear To Ear* . . . They are dressed like a couple of clowns but only the jack-o-lantern is grinning with anticipation – "Natalie" is trying to keep a "poker face" to frighten up some goodies!

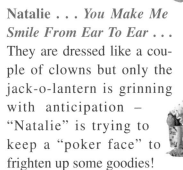

Nikki . . . *A Cold Winter's Day Won't Keep Me Away* . . . With her hat and scarf, "Nikki" is showing her "true blue" colors and qualities as a friend.

Norbit and Nyla . . . *A Friend Is Someone Who Reaches For Your Hand And Touches Your Heart* . . . Caught in the act of rubbing noses, these Arctic cubs (dated for 1999 and 2000) are cozy in fur-trimmed

parkas that are stitched with lots of love.

Norm . . . *Patience Is A Fisherman's Virtue. . .* Defying authority (note the "No Fishing" sign!), "Norm" seems content to just sit back and let nature take its course.

Paul . . . *Good Friends Warm The Heart With Many Blessings* . . . Offering a basket full of treats to his feathered friends in both a U.S. and International version, Paul is rewarded with their songs of thanks and cheery chirps in this Adoption Center Exclusive.

Randy . . . *You're Never Alone With Good Friends Around* . . . This charming teddie is the perfect companion for those times when you might be feeling a bit lonely.

Rita . . . *Wishing You Love Straight From The Heart* . . . Holding a patchwork heart bursting with love, this NALED Exclusive teddie is accompanied by her goose in a basket.

Rodney . . . *I'm Santa's Little Helper* . . . A Rudolf wanna-be, "Rodney" is ready with his volume of "Reindeer Stories" and harness lined with bells. And don't forget the plush pal who accompanies him in this Gift-To-Go Exclusive, festively packaged in a gift tin.

Roxie & Shelley . . . *What A Story We Share!* . . . In this piece, we catch two sisters reminiscing over a family scrapbook and sharing memories.

Ruth & Gene . . . *Even When We Don't See Eye To Eye, We're Always Heart To Heart* . . . This loving couple knows that an occasional disagreement is part of any healthy relationship and that true love is strong enough to overcome any obstacle.

Sally & Skip . . . *We Make A Perfect Team* . . . Catching a ride with your best friend is immortalized in this 1999 Adoption Center Exclusive, available in both a U.S. and an International version. "Sally" stands on the back of her buddy's tri-cycle as he ped-als furiously away from a scamper-ing puppy.

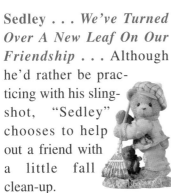

Sedley . . . *We've Turned Over A New Leaf On Our Friendship* . . . Although he'd rather be prac-ticing with his sling-shot, "Sedley" chooses to help out a friend with a little fall clean-up.

Simone & Jhodi . . . *I've Always Believed In You* . . . "Simone" was always confi-dent that her daughter would do well at the spelling bee. "Jhodi" dis-plays her prize ribbon proudly.

Skylar & Shana . . . *When You Find A Sunbeam, Share The Warmth* . . . What could be more inviting than cups of cocoa shared with a friend?

Stanley & Valerie . . . *Togetherness Is The Reason We Have Friends* . . . This couple realizes that all of their favorite playthings, stored lovingly in the chest they sit on, are useless without a good friend to enjoy them with.

Star . . . *Cherish Yesterday, Dream Tomorrow, Live Today* . . . Enjoying the sim-ple pleasures of the present, but limited to 1999 produc-tion, "Star" and friends put the finishing touches on a special holiday snowman.

Tammy . . . *Let's Go To The Hop!* . . . Dressed in her pink poodle skirt and matching sweater in this Event Exclusive, "Tammy" is practicing her moves for the next "Jukebox Jamboree!"

Teddy . . . *Friends Give You Wings To Fly* . . . "Teddy" doesn't need to look very far – his friends are always close by. His binoculars and guide book are handy, however, in case he encounters a bird of a "different" feather.

Winfield . . . *Anything Is Possible When You Wish On A Star* . . . "Winfield" and his friends look into the new millennium to get a glimpse of what the future holds. Collectors who wish to obtain this piece in the future must act fast as it is a special limited edition and will surely come and go long before the celebration is over.

ANTIQUE TOY

A Big Hug From A Little Friend . . . Often the biggest hugs come from the smallest friend – and this teddie is doing her best to show her bovine companion the depth of her affection!

Everyone Needs An Occasional Hug . . . Clutching the back of an oversized bunny on wheels, this teddie is ready to go for it!

Follow Your Heart Wherever It Takes You . . . The journey through life may not take you exactly where you planned, but this cub reminds us to take your heart along for the trip!

A Friend Is An Answered Prayer . . . Friends sometimes come to the rescue at the most unexpected times. It looks like this lamb is providing a cozy spot for his friend's nap!

A Journey With You Is One To Remember . . . Sometimes it's wise to just sit back and enjoy the ride – especially with a fun-loving friend!

Keep Good Friends Close To Your Heart . . . A "bear-to-bear" talk between friends can chase away the blues and brighten any day!

Our Friendship Is An Adventure . . . Sitting tall in the saddle can give you a different perspective on life – and the courage to start a new adventure!

You Have The Biggest Heart Of All . . . If this elephant's heart is as big as his ears, he DOES have the biggest heart of all!

BABY'S 1ST CHRISTMAS

Baby's 1st Christmas Cross . . . Complete with a baby teddie, a prayer blessing and a golden heart charm, this cross is perfect for any baby's nursery.

Baby's 1st Christmas Musical . . . Sitting on her quilt-covered building block with her bottle and locket at her feet, this charmer of a musical plays "Hush Little Baby."

Baby's 1st Christmas Nightlight . . . The soft glow given by this nightlight is sure to be a welcome sight during those 2 a.m. feedings.

Baby's 1st Christmas Photo Frame Ornament . . . A hanging ornament featuring a baby teddie sitting upon a white ruffled frame provides the perfect spot for baby's portrait.

Baby's 1st Christmas Rattle and Spoon Ornaments . . . This pair of ornaments gives collectors another option when shopping for the new baby in the family.

Bianca . . . *Sweet Dreams My Little One* . . . Cute as a button in a white sweater and matching hat, this general figurine complements this series perfectly.

BEARY-GO-ROUND CAROUSEL

Archie . . . *Through Ups And Downs, You're Still The Best Friend Around* . . . Dressed in matching clown accessories, this duo looks like their off to the circus!

Bill . . . *Friends Like You Are Always True Blue* . . . Carrying his flag proudly, "Bill" strikes a brave bruin pose.

Cody . . . *I'll Cherish You For Many Moons* . . . Donning American Indian garb, this teddie rides his palomino pony like the wind!

Crystal . . . *Hang On! We're In For A Wonderful Ride* . . . A magical unicorn gives winged "Crystal" a spin!

Crystal (Rare Bear) . . . *Hang On! We're In For A Wonderful Ride* . . . The message of friendship is crystal-clear in this rare version. Collectors, hang on for the ride of your life!

Flossie . . . *I'd Stick My Neck Out For You Anytime* . . . This giraffe has plenty of neck to stick out for her lucky friends!

Gina . . . *Where Friends Gather, Magic Blossoms* . . . All dressed up in red, white and blue, "Gina" could stay on the merry-go-round all day!

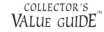

Ivan . . . *I've Packed My Trunk And I'm Ready To Go* . . . "Have ice cream, will travel!" Ivan has all of life's little necessities in hand!

Jason . . . *When It Comes To Friendship, You've Really Earned Your Stripes* . . . With the stripes of a hero, this zebra carries his rider off on yet another adventure.

Jenelle . . . *A Friend Is Somebunny To Cherish Forever* . . . Decked out for spring, a happy "Jenelle" and friend are off to the carrot patch!

Jerrod . . . *Don't Worry – It's Just Another Little Bump In The Road* . . . Who knows more about bumps than a friendly camel?

Marcus . . . *There's Nobody I'd Rather Go 'Round With Than You* . . . A ride from a reindeer? Sure! Santa does it all the time!

Virginia . . . *It's So Merry Going 'Round With You* . . . Blooms adorn this horse and rider in hues of pink and blue.

HAPPILY EVER AFTER

Pinocchio . . . *You've Got My Heart On A String* . . . This rendition of a classic tale about a wooden boy who comes to life is a must-have for collectors of the ongoing *Happily Ever After* series.

Winnie . . . *You're My Perfect Prince* . . . You can often find your Prince Charming in the most unlikely places. Keep your eyes open!

LET HEAVEN AND NATURE SING

Felicia . . . *Joy To The World* . . . Limited to one year of production, the first issue in this series shows

teddie "Felicia" strolling with a friendly little lamb.

OLD FASHIONED COUNTRY CHRISTMAS

Annette . . . *Tender Care Given Here* . . . All tuckered out from her holiday shopping, "Annette" tenderly cradles her tree and holly while sitting down for a spell.

Brian . . . *Look Out Snow! Here We Go!* . . . Brian and his friends are all bundled up and ready to go on a much anticipated sleigh ride! Giddyap!

Country Christmas Accessories . . . After a day of holiday shopping and decorating, your *Old Fashioned Country Christmas* figurines need a place to hang their hat, sit down for a minute and admire their handiwork. These pieces provide just that – a coat rack, a rocking chair and a tiny decorated tree atop a chest of drawers.

Justin . . . *We Share Forever, Whatever The Weather* . . . Although he got caught in a storm, "Justin" trudges in with the best tree on the lot!

Shirley . . . *These Are The Best Kind Of Days* . . . Although it can be frantic, gathering holiday decorations for her home is the best part of "Shirley's" day.

Suzanne . . . *Home Sweet Country Home* . . . For "Suzanne," the best part of the holidays is watching the snow transform *Cherished Teddies Town*!

OUR CHERISHED DAY

A Beary Special Groom-To-Be . . . This bruin anxiously looks at his pocket watch, counting down the last few moments until he will make this

beautiful woman his wife. He can hardly wait to kiss the bride!

Beautiful and Bearly Blushing . . . Looking radiant in her gown, this beauty glows in anticipation of spending the rest of her life with the man she loves.

I've Got The Most Important Job! . . . "Bearing" the wedding rings is a job given to the most trusted teddie in town!

Our Cherished Wedding Collectors Set . . . A symbol of shared memories, or of dreams to come, this set of newlyweds is perfect for any true romantic.

So Glad To Be Part Of Your Special Day . . . Handkerchief in hand, this bridesmaid in blue is ready for the inevitable tears of joy!

Sweet Flowers For The Bride . . . This little girl is proud to serve the blushing bride on her special day.

The Time Has Come For Wedding Bliss . . . On hand to witness the vows of his friend, this groomsman has a corsage for his favorite girl.

SANTA SERIES

Sanford . . . *Celebrate Family, Friends And Tradition* . . . Hanging the stockings by the chimney with care is "Sanford's" favorite way to prepare for the holidays. This detailed piece is the 1999 edition in the *Santa Series*.

SCHOOL DAYS

School Days Mini Figurines . . . *Boy In Baseball Hat* . . . This star player would much rather spend this season out on the field than in the classroom.

School Days Mini Figurines *. . . Boy With Book And Apple . . .* With an apple for his teacher and a book in his arm, this teddie is ready to become the star pupil!

School Days Mini Figurines *. . . Girl With Apple And Flag . . .* Pick up this tiny teddie and you'll perk up your day with some of her infectious school spirit!

School Days Mini Figurines . . . *Girl With Pom Poms . . .* Give me a T! Give me an E! Give me a D-D-I-E-S!!! Go, Teddies!!

School Days Plaque . . . Show your favorite teacher how much you appreciate her with this piece from the *School Days* series.

TEDDIE TRIUMPHS

  This series features teddies with different messages of encourage-

ment and success. Making their debut are: **"Awesome!," "Congratulations," "Good Job," "I'm Proud Of You," "Keep Trying"** and **"You Did It."**

TEDDIES IN MOTION

This new series zooms in to join the rest of the 1999 releases. The pieces feature cars from the good ol' days and one even features a limited edition fire truck!

UP IN THE ATTIC

Sarah . . . *Memories To Wear And Share . . .* This 1999 addition to the *Up In The Attic* series features a little lady who knows that clothes do more than just keep you warm. With her little fashion critic looking over her shoulder, "Sarah" is sure to pick out the perfect ensemble.

CANDLEHOLDERS

Burning up the season on the **Cherished Teddies** scene are the **"Bear Sitting**

Candleholder" (set/2) and "Christmas Tealight Candleholder." These pieces are sure to leave any collector glowing.

EGGS

New for 1999 are three Easter eggs, with a choice of a green, pink or yellow bow. Featured are teddies bearing baskets full of colorful eggs and flowers.

FRAMES

Wedding Photo Frame . . . Sitting among a border of daisies, these newlyweds will complement a photo of your own special day!

MUSICALS

Wedding Action Musical . . . Relive your

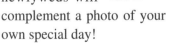

walk down the aisle in this revolving musical. The musical plays "Mendelssohn's Wedding March."

ORNAMENTS

Celebrate the new year and the millennium with "Eskimos Holding Fish" (set/2, Dated 1999 and 2000) as our neighbors to the north are celebrating the first and last years of the centuries in this charming duo of ornaments. And bring on the holiday cheer with a colorful assortment of "Bears With Hats/Scarfs" that are sure to keep the chill out of any heart.

PLAQUES

The new releases in the plaque category are a perfect way to keep track of life's memorable milestones. The spring releases include: "Baby Girl With Lamb," "Birthday Bear," "Boy Graduate," "Bride And Groom," "Girl And Boy With Kite" and

"Girls With Teddies And Cookies." While a new assortment of mini seasonal plaques allow you to bring a sense of love and warmth into your home with "Bear In Hat And Scarf," "Bear In Santa Suit" and "Bear With Puppy."

PLATES

Eskimos Holding Stars . . . Two Eskimos holding golden stars are sharing a secret in this frosty glass plate dated 1999 and 2000. Collectors should act fast before this limited edition is no longer available.

STOCKING HOLDERS

Boy With Holly . . . Holly leaves, berries and pine cones provide the base for this festive stocking holder.

GENERAL PLUSH

A number of adorable bean bag teddies make their debut in 1999. While designs range from plush versions of the resin figurines, "Jacki," "Karen" and "Sara" to a plethora of plush exclusives, this new cast of characters is sure to delight collectors.

HOLIDAY OCCASIONS PLUSH

Celebrate the special days of the year, as well as the special people in your life with this new series of teddies. From "Halloween" to "Teacher," these pieces will make any occasion memorable.

MONTHLY PLUSH

Each of the 12 months are honored in this new series. Each piece features a heart on its chest in the color of the month's birthstone.

T-SHIRT TEDDIES

The perfect way to send a big bear hug is through one of the new *T-Shirt Teddies* plush bears.

*T*he **Cherished Teddies** line began it all for Priscilla Hillman in 1992, but she didn't stop with the bears! Almost every year since, the prolific artist has introduced a new line of collectibles featuring other animals and more!

SPOTLIGHT

Calico Kittens® – Introduced in 1993, this feline-inspired line of collectibles offers a wide range of choices for cat-lovers looking for the "purr-fect" piece to add to their collection

Priscilla's Mouse Tales™ – When Hillman realized her cats had nothing to chase, a new line of mice was brought to the Enesco family of collectibles. Introduced in 1995, these figurines re-create the nursery rhyme illustrations that Hillman created before she joined Enesco in the early 1980s.

My Blushing Bunnies™ – Hillman's love of the outdoors and her affection for woodland animals led her to create this adorable line of rabbits, who joined the Hillman teddies, kittens and mice in 1996. Although these cuties are caught in a variety of unnatural poses (bunnies don't brush their teeth, do they?), their realistic features are a favorite of their creator.

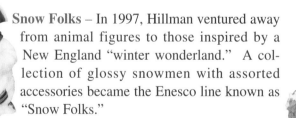

Snow Folks – In 1997, Hillman ventured away from animal figures to those inspired by a New England "winter wonderland." A collection of glossy snowmen with assorted accessories became the Enesco line known as "Snow Folks."

Down Petticoat Lane – This 1998 introduction from Priscilla Hillman offers a world of friendship with its dolls and teddies that are sure to invoke memories of days gone by.

COLLECTOR'S CLUB NEWS

CLUB NEWS

*H*appy anniversary to *The Cherished Teddies Club*! This year marks the 5th anniversary for the club, which has become one of the largest in the country with a "membearship" of almost 200,000. And if you're already a membear, you know the many joys the club has to offer. If you're not a membear yet however, there's no better time to join than now.

Sign Me Up!

To become a membear of *The Cherished Teddies Club*, just visit your local Cherished Teddies retailer for an application, or write to Enesco at:

The Cherished Teddies Club
P.O. Box 219
Itasca, IL 60143-0219
1-800-NEAR-YOU
(1-800-632-7968)

You can also join on the Internet at www.enesco.com. Go to the Club page for directions!

Membearship to *The Cherished Teddies Club* is $20 and entitles you to a full year of exciting benefits! Upon joining the club, you'll receive "Lanny," the 1999 Membearship Figurine, who's just one of five pieces that make up the anniversary parade. The other four characters are available for purchase to march alongside the "1999 Membears Only Float" are "Letty," "Vivienne" and "Walter."

As a club membear, you'll also receive a sculpted lapel pin, a special "Exclusive 5th Anniversary Mini Figurine," a subscription to *The Town Tattler* which will keep you informed of all the **Cherished Teddies** info you need to know, a color catalog and access to the exclusive *The Cherished Teddies Club* web site!

RECENT RETIREMENTS & SUSPENSIONS

*T*his section highlights the 12 **Cherished Teddies** figurines that were retired, effective February 27, 1999. Limited editions become "closed" when the piece's edition quantity or time period runs out. Each piece's issue year and stock number is in parentheses.

- ❏ Allison & Alexandria (1995, #127981)
- ❏ Hunter (1998, #354104)
- ❏ Madeline (1995, #135593)
- ❏ Margaret (1995, #103667)
- ❏ Marie (1993, #910767)
- ❏ Marilyn (1995, #135682)
- ❏ Patrice (1993, #911429)
- ❏ Patrick (1993, #911410)
- ❏ Robert (1996, #156272)
- ❏ Seth & Sarabeth (1995, #128015)
- ❏ Tracie and Nicole (1993, #911372)
- ❏ Violet (1996, #156280)

FOR A LIMITED TIME ONLY!

Here are the 1999 **Cherished Teddies** limited edition figurines. Some of the pieces are available at your local store, others, however, may only be obtained at special events or through selected outlets and are noted below with an asterisk (*).

- ❏ Alex (#368156)*
- ❏ Anita (#477915)*
- ❏ Ava (#546526)*
- ❏ Bette (#533637)*
- ❏ Crystal (#589942R, *Cherished Teddies Carousel*)*
- ❏ Daisy & Chelsea (#597392)*
- ❏ Dennis (#510963)*
- ❏ Dustin and Austin (#477508, *Teddies In Motion*)
- ❏ Ed (#466220)*
- ❏ Felicia (#533890, *Let Heaven And Nature Sing*)
- ❏ Follow The Yellow Brick Road Collector Set (#476501)
- ❏ Glenn (#477893)
- ❏ Graduation (#477907)*
- ❏ If A Mom's Love Comes Comes In All Sizes, Yours Has The Biggest Of Hearts (#302988)
- ❏ Jasmine (#202940)*
- ❏ Jerome (#546534)*

- ❏ Katie, Renee, Jessica, Matthew (#538299)*
- ❏ Kayla (#533815)*
- ❏ Matt and Vicki (#476781)
- ❏ Norbit and Nyla (#534188)
- ❏ Paul (#466328)*
- ❏ Paul (#466328I)*
- ❏ Rita (#476617)*
- ❏ Rodney (#533882)*
- ❏ Sally & Skip (#510955)
- ❏ Sally & Skip (#510955F)
- ❏ Sanford (#534242)
- ❏ Sarah (#308676, *Up In The Attic*)
- ❏ Star (#534250)
- ❏ Tammy (#510947)*

CHERISHED TEDDIES® TOP TEN

*T*his section highlights the ten most valuable **Cherished Teddies** figurines, as determined by their values on the secondary market. In order to qualify for this section, the piece must have top dollar value and show an increase in value from its original price.

Daisy (#910651)
Issued 1993 – Retired 1996
Original Price: $15
Secondary Market Value: **Letter – $850**
Market Meter: +5,567%

Chelsea (#910694)
Issued 1993 – Retired 1995
Original Price: $15
Secondary Market Value: **Letter – $320**
Market Meter: +2,033%

Holding On To Someone Special (#916285)
Issued 1993 – Closed 1993
Original Price: $20
Secondary Market Value: **No Mark – $270**
Market Meter: +1,250%

Charity (#910678)
Issued 1993 – Retired 1996
Original Price: $20
Secondary Market Value: **Letter – $265**
Market Meter: +1,225%

Priscilla Ann (1994-95 Expo Exclusive, #CRT025)
Issued 1994 – Closed 1995
Original Price: $25
Secondary Market Value: **4-mark – $260**
Market Meter: +940%

Alice (#912875)
Issued 1993 – Closed 1993
Original Price: $17.50
Secondary Market Value: **3-Mark – $228**
Market Meter: +1,203%

Theodore, Samantha & Tyler (9", #912883)
Issued 1993 – Suspended 1995
Original Price: $160
Secondary Market Value: **3-Mark – $225**
Market Meter: +41%

Tasha (International Exclusive, #156353F)
Issued 1996 – Closed 1996
Original Price: N/A
Secondary Market Value: **No Mark – $220**
Market Meter: N/A

Teddy and Roosevelt (#624918)
Issued 1993 – Closed 1993
Original Price: $20
Secondary Market Value: **3-Mark– $215**
Market Meter: +975%

Beth and Blossom (#950564)
Variation: with butterfly
Issued 1992 – Retired 1997
Original Price: $50
Secondary Market Value: **Letter – $210**
Market Meter: +320%

How To Use Your Collector's Value Guide™

1. Locate your piece in the Value Guide. The pieces are listed alphabetically with general figurines listed first, followed by figurine series (listed alphabetically by series name). Other **Cherished Teddies** collectibles (frames, ornaments, plates, etc.) come next and the section concludes with plush and club exclusives. Seasonal pieces are listed in the general figurines section and are marked with symbols denoting the appropriate theme. Handy alphabetical and numerical indexes can be found in the back of the book. Note: some items pictured are prototypes and may differ slightly from the actual piece.

② #900362 ❀

Abigail
Inside We're All The Same
Issued: 1993 • Suspended: 1995
Original Price: $16
Value by Year Mark:
LETTER–$98 **3**–$60 **4**–$52

2. Look at the handwritten registration number on the bottom of your piece. The first number or letter of this registration number is considered the **year mark**.

3. Find the market value which corresponds with the year mark on the bottom of your piece. For pieces produced without year marks or with undetermined year marks, only one value is listed. Pieces for which a secondary market value is not established are listed with values as "N/E." Pieces that were suspended, but were returned to production are noted with a triangle (Δ) after their status information.

FIGURINES	
Price Paid	Value Of My Collection
1.	
2. *16*	*60*
3.	
4.	
5.	
16	*60*
PENCIL TOTALS	

4. Record the original price that you paid and the current market value of the piece in the boxes at the bottom of each Value Guide page.

5. Calculate the value for the page by adding all of the boxes in each column. Then, transfer the totals from each page to the "Total Value Of My Collection" worksheets on pages 161-162. Add all of the totals together to determine the overall value of your collection. Use a pencil so you can change the totals as your collection grows!

SEASONAL SYMBOLS	
♥ Valentine's Day	🎃 Halloween
♣ St. Patrick's Day	🦃 Thanksgiving
❀ Spring/Easter	🌲 Winter/Christmas

GENERAL FIGURINES

In 1992, the first **Cherished Teddies** pieces were introduced to collectors who immediately took them into their hearts and homes. Since then, nearly 300 figurines of these charming teddies have been produced, including 66 new items for 1999. Waiting to be adopted this year, the new designs can "bearly" control themselves, anticipating their journey to a loving home. Themes of the old and familiar are again popular, but the 1999 **Cherished Teddies** releases are also looking forward to the future with the advent of the new millennium at the end of the year. Collectors should not have difficulty finding the perfect additions for their growing group of growlers!

① #302708

25 Years To Treasure Together
Issued: 1998 • Current
Original Price: $30
Value by Year Mark:
7–$30 **8**–$30 **9**–$30

② #900362

Abigail
Inside We're All The Same
Issued: 1993 • Suspended: 1995
Original Price: $16
Value by Year Mark:
LETTER–$98 **3**–$60 **4**–$52

③ #103594

Aiming For Your Heart
Issued: 1995 • Suspended: 1995
Original Price: $25
Value by Year Mark: **4**–$48

④ #368156
New!

Alex
(1999 Event Exclusive)
Cherish The Little Things
Issued: 1999
To Be Closed: 1999
Original Price: $17.50
Value by Year Mark: **9**–$17.50

⑤ #903620

Alice (9")
Cozy Warm Wishes
Coming Your Way
Issued: 1993 • Suspended: 1995
Original Price: $100
Value by Year Mark:
3–$188 **4**–$155

FIGURINES		
	Price Paid	Value Of My Collection
1.		
2.		
3.		
4.		
5.		
PENCIL TOTALS		

① #912875

Alice (Dated 1993)
Cozy Warm Wishes
Coming Your Way
Issued: 1993 • Closed: 1993
Original Price: $17.50
Value by Year Mark: **3**–$228

② #127981

Allison & Alexandria
Two Friends Mean
Twice The Love
Issued: 1995 • Retired: 1999
Original Price: $25
Value by Year Mark:
4–$50 **5**–$42 **6**–$32
7–$29 **8**–$27 **9**–$27

③ #533866

New!

Alyssa
You Warm My Soul
Issued: 1999 • Current
Original Price: $15
Value by Year Mark:
8–$15 **9**–$15

④ #141186

Amanda (Dated 1995)
Here's Some Cheer To
Last The Year
Issued: 1995 • Closed: 1995
Original Price: $17.50
Value by Year Mark: **5**–$52

⑤ #910732

Amy
Hearts Quilted With Love
Issued: 1993 • Current
Original Price: $13.50
Value by Year Mark:
***LETTER**–$65 **3**–$49 **4**–$37 **5**–$33
6–$30 **7**–$20 **8**–$15 **9**–$15*
Variation: with lavender bow
Value: $62

⑥ #176265

Andy
You Have A Special
Place In My Heart
Issued: 1996 • Retired: 1998
Original Price: $18.50
Value by Year Mark:
6–$34 **7**–$25 **8**–$21

FIGURINES

	Price Paid	Value Of My Collection
1.		
2.		
3.		
4.	17.50	52.00
5.		
6.		
7.		
8.		
	17.50	52.00

PENCIL TOTALS

⑦ #477915

New!

Anita
(1999 Catalog Exclusive)
You're A Tulip To Treasure
Issued: 1999
To Be Closed: 1999
Original Price: $20
Value by Year Mark: **9**–$20

⑧ #950459

Anna
Hooray For You
Issued: 1992 • Retired: 1997
Original Price: $22.50
Value by Year Mark:
***LETTER**–$98 **3**–$77 **4**–$58
5–$48 **6**–$42 **7**–$36*

FIGURINES

① #534234

New!

Anne
So Glad You're Here To Keep Me Warm
Issued: 1999 • Current
Original Price: $10
Value by Year Mark:
8–$10 **9**–$10

② #205354

Annie, Brittany, Colby, Danny and Ernie (5th Anniversary Piece, LE-1997)
Strike Up The Band And Give Five Cherished Years A Hand
Issued: 1997 • Closed: 1997
Original Price: $75
Value by Year Mark: **7**–$80

③ #476978

New!

Anxiously Awaiting The Arrival
Issued: 1999 • Current
Original Price: $15
Value by Year Mark:
8–$15 **9**–$15

④ #476161

New!

Arnold
You "Putt" Me In A Great Mood
Issued: 1999 • Current
Original Price: $17.50
Value by Year Mark:
8–$17.50 **9**–$17.50

⑤ #546526

New!

Ava
(1999 Avon Exclusive)
You Make Me Feel Beautiful Inside
Issued: 1999
To Be Closed: 1999
Original Price: $19.99
Value by Year Mark: **9**–$19.99

⑥ #203874

Baby With Diaper Shelf Sitter
Issued: 1997 • Current
Original Price: $30
Value by Year Mark:
7–$30 **8**–$30 **9**–$30

⑦ #270016

Barry
I'm Batty Over You
Issued: 1997 • Current
Original Price: $17.50
Value by Year Mark:
7–$25 **8**–$17.50 **9**–$17.50

⑧ #103586

Be My Bow
Issued: 1995 • Suspended: 1995
Original Price: $15
Value by Year Mark: **4**–$47

	FIGURINES	
	Price Paid	Value Of My Collection
1.		
2.		
3.		
4.		
5.		
6.		
7.		
8.		
	PENCIL TOTALS	

FIGURINES

1 — #141348

Bea
"Bee" My Friend
Issued: 1995 • Retired: 1998
Original Price: $15
Value by Year Mark:
5–$32 **6**–$24 **7**–$22 **8**–$19

2 — #916331

Becky
Springtime Happiness
Issued: 1994 • Suspended: 1995
Original Price: $20
Value by Year Mark:
3–$73 **4**–$62

3 — #950548

Benji
Life Is Sweet, Enjoy
Issued: 1992
Suspended: 1995 • Retired: 1995
Original Price: $13.50
Value by Year Mark:
LETTER–$80 **3**–$58 **4**–$50

4 — #163457

Bertie
(International Exclusive)
Friends Forever Near Or Far
Issued: 1995 • Current
Original Price: N/A
Value by Year Mark:
5–$58 **6**–$42 **7**–$35
8–N/E **9**–N/E

5 — #916404

Bessie
Some Bunny Loves You
Issued: 1994 • Suspended: 1995
Original Price: $15
Value by Year Mark:
3–$200 **4**–$180

6 — #127949

The Best Is Yet To Come
Issued: 1995 • Current
Original Price: $12.50
Value by Year Mark:
4–$32 **5**–$26 **6**–$18
7–$15 **8**–$13.50 **9**–$13.50

FIGURINES

	Price Paid	Value Of My Collection
1.		
2.		
3.		
4.		
5.	15.00	200.00
6.		
7.		
8.		
	15.00	200.00

PENCIL TOTALS

7 — #127957

The Best Is Yet To Come
Issued: 1995 • Current
Original Price: $12.50
Value by Year Mark:
4–$28 **5**–$24 **6**–$17
7–$15 **8**–$13.50 **9**–$13.50

8 — #950637

Beth
Bear Hugs
Issued: 1992
Suspended: 1995 • Retired: 1995
Original Price: $17.50
Value by Year Mark:
LETTER–$92 **3**–$75 **4**–$65

① #950807

Beth
Happy Holidays, Deer Friend
Issued: 1992 • Suspended: 1995
Original Price: $22.50
Value by Year Mark:
LETTER–$90 **3**–$76
4–$68 **5**–$58

② #950564

Beth and Blossom
Friends Are Never Far Apart
Issued: 1992 • Retired: 1997
Original Price: $50
Value by Year Mark:
3–$92 **4**–$82 **5**–$75 **6**–$70
Variation: with butterfly
Value by Year Mark:
LETTER–$210 **3**–$180

③ #624896

Betsey
The First Step To Love
Issued: 1994 • Current
Original Price: $12.50
Value by Year Mark:
3–$35 **4**–$30 **5**–$23 **6**–$18
7–$14 **8**–$12.50 **9**–$12.50

④ #533637

New!

Bette
(1999 Adoption Center
Event Exclusive)
You Are The Star Of The Show
Issued: 1999
To Be Closed: 1999
Original Price: $20
Value by Year Mark: **9**–$20

⑤ #626066

Betty
Bubblin' Over With Love
Issued: 1994 • Current
Original Price: $18.50
Value by Year Mark:
3–$58 **4**–$49 **5**–$42 **6**–$30
7–$22 **8**–$20 **9**–$20

⑥ #624896

Billy
Everyone Needs A Cuddle
Issued: 1994 • Current
Original Price: $12.50
Value by Year Mark:
3–$42 **4**–$33 **5**–$24 **6**–$21
7–$15 **8**–$12.50 **9**–$12.50
Variation: spelled "Billie"
Value: $58

⑦ #624896

Bobbie
A Little Friendship To Share
Issued: 1994 • Current
Original Price: $12.50
Value by Year Mark:
3–$42 **4**–$29 **5**–$24 **6**–$18
7–$15 **8**–$12.50 **9**–$12.50

⑧ #466301

Bonnie and Harold
Ring In The Holidays With Me
Issued: 1998 • Current
Original Price: $25
Value by Year Mark:
8–$25 **9**–$25

FIGURINES		
	Price Paid	Value Of My Collection
1.		
2.		
3.		
4.		
5.	18.50	42.00
6.		
7.		
8.		
	18.50	42.00
PENCIL TOTALS		

① #869082

Boy And Girl Cupid
Heart To Heart
Issued: 1995 • Suspended: 1995
Original Price: $18.50
Value by Year Mark: **4**–$44

② #869082

Boy And Girl Cupid
My Love
Issued: 1995 • Suspended: 1995
Original Price: $18.50
Value by Year Mark: **4**–$44

③ #869074

Boy Cupid
From My Heart
Issued: 1995 • Suspended: 1995
Original Price: $13.50
Value by Year Mark: **4**–$40

④ #869074

Boy Cupid
Sealed With Love
Issued: 1995 • Suspended: 1995
Original Price: $13.50
Value by Year Mark: **4**–$40

⑤ #354252

Brandon
Friendship Is My Goal
Issued: 1998 • Current
Original Price: $20
Value by Year Mark:
8–$20 **9**–$20

⑥ #617180

Breanna
Pumpkin Patch Pals
Issued: 1994 • Retired: 1998
Original Price: $15
Value by Year Mark:
4–$54 **5**–$42 **6**–$29
7–$22 **8**–$18

	FIGURINES	
	Price Paid	Value Of My Collection
1.		
2.	18.50	44.00
3.		
4.		
5.		
6.		
7.		
8.		
	18.50	44.00
	PENCIL TOTALS	

⑦ #912816

Brenda
How I Love Being Friends With You
Issued: 1993
Suspended: 1995 • Retired: 1995
Original Price: $15
Value by Year Mark:
3–$75 **4**–$53 **5**–$45

⑧ #302686

Brooke
Arriving With Love And Care
Issued: 1998 • Current
Original Price: $25
Value by Year Mark:
7–$27 **8**–$25 **9**–$25

FIGURINES

① #912816

Buckey
*How I Love Being
Friends With You*
Issued: 1993
Suspended: 1995 • Retired: 1995
Original Price: $15
Value by Year Mark:
3–$75 **4**–$60 **5**–$52

② #103802

Bunny
Just In Time For Spring
Issued: 1995 • Retired: 1998 ∆
Original Price: $13.50
Value by Year Mark:
4–$32 **5**–$25 **6**–$18
7–$15 **8**–$13.50

③ #156388

Butch
Can I Be Your Football Hero?
Issued: 1996 • Current
Original Price: $15
Value by Year Mark:
5–$30 **6**–$22 **7**–$18
8–$15 **9**–$15

④ #950424

Camille
I'd Be Lost Without You
Issued: 1992 • Retired: 1996
Original Price: $20
Value by Year Mark:
LETTER–$78 **3**–$55 **4**–$42
5–$34 **6**–$32

⑤ #215856

**Can't Bear To See You
Under The Weather**
Issued: 1997 • Current
Original Price: $15
Value by Year Mark:
7–$22 **8**–$15 **9**–$15

⑥ #533874

New!

Carlin & Janay
*When I Count My Blessings,
I Count You Twice*
Issued: 1999 • Current
Original Price: $25
Value by Year Mark:
8–$25 **9**–$25

⑦ #352969

Carol
Angels Snow How To Fly
Issued: 1998 • Current
Original Price: $17.50
Value by Year Mark:
8–$17.50 **9**–$17.50

⑧ #912921

Carolyn
Wishing You All Good Things
Issued: 1993
Suspended: 1996 • Retired: 1996
Original Price: $22.50
Value by Year Mark:
3–$70 **4**–$56 **5**–$44 **6**–$37

	Price Paid	Value Of My Collection
FIGURINES		
1.		
2.		
3.		
4.		
5.		
6.		
7.		
8.		
PENCIL TOTALS		

① #141321

Carrie
The Future "Beareth" All Things
Issued: 1995 • Retired: 1998
Original Price: $18.50
Value by Year Mark:
5–$38 **6**–$27 **7**–$23 **8**–$20

② #269980

Cathy
An Autumn Breeze Blows
Blessings To Please
Issued: 1997 • Current
Original Price: $25
Value by Year Mark:
7–$32 **8**–$25 **9**–$25

③ #601578

New!

Charissa & Ashylynn
Every Journey Begins
With One Step
Issued: 1999 • Current
Original Price: $25
Value by Year Mark:
8–$25 **9**–$25

④ #910678

Charity
I Found A Friend In Ewe
Issued: 1993
Suspended: 1994 • Retired: 1996
Original Price: $20
Value by Year Mark:
LETTER–$265 **3**–$230

⑤ #950742

Charlie
The Spirit Of Friendship
Warms The Heart
Issued: 1992
Suspended: 1996 • Retired: 1996
Original Price: $22.50
Value by Year Mark:
LETTER–$76 **3**–$65 **4**–$60 **5**–$52

⑥ #910694

Chelsea
Good Friends Are A Blessing
Issued: 1993
Suspended: 1995 • Retired: 1995
Original Price: $15
Value by Year Mark:
LETTER–$320 **3**–$280 **4**–$270

FIGURINES

	Price Paid	Value Of My Collection
1.		
2.		
3.		
4.		
5.		
6.		
7.		
8.		

PENCIL TOTALS

⑦ #476633

New!

Cherish
Reach Out To Someone
Around You
Issued: 1999 • Current
Original Price: $12.50
Value by Year Mark:
8–$12.50 **9**–$12.50

⑧ #CRT109

Cherished Teddies Town
Sign (1995 Event Exclusive)
Issued: 1995 • Closed: 1995
Original Price: $6
Value: $22

1 · #141216

Cheryl and Carl
Wishing You A Cozy Christmas
Issued: 1996 • Retired: 1998
Original Price: $25
Value by Year Mark:
6–$35 **7**–$29 **8**–$27

2 · #103837

Christian
My Prayer Is For You
Issued: 1995 • Current
Original Price: $18.50
Value by Year Mark:
4–$33 **5**–$30 **6**–$25
7–$20 **8**–$18.50 **9**–$18.50

3 · #103845

Christine
My Prayer Is For You
Issued: 1995 • Current
Original Price: $18.50
Value by Year Mark:
4–$33 **5**–$30 **6**–$25
7–$20 **8**–$18.50 **9**–$18.50

4 · #950483

Christopher
Old Friends Are The Best Friends
Issued: 1992 • Current
Original Price: $50
Value by Year Mark:
LETTER–$120 **3**–$90
4–$80 **5**–$72 **6**–$62
7–$58 **8**–$50 **9**–$50

5 · #128023

Christy
Take Me To Your Heart
Issued: 1995 • Retired: 1996
Original Price: $12.50
Value by Year Mark:
4–$58 **5**–$49 **6**–$45
Variation: white ribbon with blue dots
Value by Year Mark: **5**–$68

6 · #912794

Connie
You're A Sweet Treat
Issued: 1993
Suspended: 1996 • Retired: 1996
Original Price: $15
Value by Year Mark:
3–$48 **4**–$40 **5**–$33

7 · #916390

Courtney
*Springtime Is A Blessing
From Above*
Issued: 1994
Suspended: 1995 • Retired: 1996
Original Price: $15
Value by Year Mark:
3–$160 **4**–$132 **5**–$114

8 · #910651

Daisy
Friendship Blossoms With Love
Issued: 1993
Suspended: 1995 • Retired: 1996
Original Price: $15
Value by Year Mark:
LETTER–$850 **3**–$800

	Price Paid	Value Of My Collection
FIGURINES		
1.		
2.		
3.		
4.		
5.		
6.		
7.		
8.		
PENCIL TOTALS		

① #597392

New!

Daisy & Chelsea
(1999 Event Exclusive)
Old Friends Always Find
Their Way Back
Issued: 1999
To Be Closed: 1999
Original Price: $20 (w/purchase)
Value by Year Mark: **9**–$20

② #176214

Daniel
You're My Little Pumpkin
Issued: 1996 • Retired: 1998
Original Price: $22.50
Value by Year Mark:
6–$42 **7**–$29 **8**–$25

③ #265780

Danielle, Sabrina, Tiffany
(1997 Adoption Center
Exclusive, LE-25,000)
We're Three Of A Kind
Issued: 1997 • Closed: 1997
Original Price: $35
Value by Year Mark: **7**–$73

④ #265780F

Danielle, Sabrina, Tiffany
(1997 International
Adoption Center
Exclusive, LE-17,500)
We're Three Of A Kind
Issued: 1997 • Closed: 1997
Original Price: N/A
Value by Year Mark: **7**–$88

⑤ #156361

Debbie
Let's Hear It For Friendship!
Issued: 1996 • Current
Original Price: $15
Value by Year Mark:
6–$28 **7**–$20 **8**–$15 **9**–$15

⑥ #302694

A Decade Of Teddy
Bear Love
Issued: 1998 • Current
Original Price: $30
Value by Year Mark:
7–$30 **8**–$30 **9**–$30

FIGURINES		
	Price Paid	Value Of My Collection
1.		
2.		
3.		
4.		
5.		
6.		
7.		
8.		
PENCIL TOTALS		

⑦ #510963

New!

Dennis
(1999 Event Exclusive)
You Put The Spice In My Life
Issued: 1999
To Be Closed: 1999
Original Price: $17.50
Value by Year Mark: **9**–$17.50

⑧ #103799

Donald
Friends Are Egg-ceptional Blessings
Issued: 1995
Suspended: 1995 • Retired: 1998
Original Price: $20
Value by Year Mark:
4–$50 **5**–$38 **6**–$29
7–$24 **8**–$20

① #128023

Dorothy
Love Me True
Issued: 1995 • Retired: 1996
Original Price: $12.50
Value by Year Mark:
4–$60 **5**–$47 **6**–$35
Variation: white ribbon with yellow dots
Value by Year Mark: **5**–$66

② #950661

Douglas
Let's Be Friends
Issued: 1992
Suspended: 1995 • Retired: 1995
Original Price: $20
Value by Year Mark:
LETTER–$120 **3**–$98 **4**–$86

③ #163473

Duncan
(International Exclusive)
Your Friendship Is Music To My Ears
Issued: 1995 • Current
Original Price: N/A
Value by Year Mark:
5–$64 **6**–$44 **7**–$35
8–N/E **9**–N/E

④ #131873

Earl
Warm Hearted Friends
Issued: 1995 • Retired: 1998
Original Price: $17.50
Value by Year Mark:
5–$39 **6**–$27 **7**–$23 **8**–$20

⑤ #466220 New!

Ed
(1999 Event Exclusive)
There's A Patch In My Heart For You
Issued: 1999
To Be Closed: 1999
Original Price: $20
Value by Year Mark: **9**–$20

⑥ #916277

Elizabeth & Ashley
My Beary Best Friend
Issued: 1994
Suspended: 1995 • Retired: 1996
Original Price: $25
Value by Year Mark:
3–$82 **4**–$72

⑦ #622796

Eric
Bear Tidings Of Joy
Issued: 1994 • Retired: 1998
Original Price: $22.50
Value by Year Mark:
4–$42 **5**–$38 **6**–$31
7–$28 **8**–$27

⑧ #176028

Erica
Friends Are Always Pulling For You
Issued: 1996 • Current
Original Price: $22.50
Value by Year Mark:
6–$32 **7**–$26
8–$22.50 **9**–$22.50

FIGURINES

	Price Paid	Value Of My Collection
1.		
2.		
3.		
4.	17.50	39.00
5.		
6.		
7.	22.50	38.00
8.	22.50	32.00
	62.50	109.00

PENCIL TOTALS

(1) #203068

Erin
*My Irish Eyes Smile
When You're Near*
Issued: 1998 • Current
Original Price: $15
Value by Year Mark:
8–$15 **9**–$15

(2) #916412

Faith
There's No Bunny Like You
Issued: 1994 • Suspended: 1995
Original Price: $20
Value by Year Mark:
3–$80 **4**–$70 **5**–$62

(3) #476684

New!

Fay & Arlene
*Thanks For Always Being
By My Side*
Issued: 1999 • Current
Original Price: $25
Value by Year Mark:
8–$25 **9**–$25

(4) #476501

New!

Scott Tim Leo Dot

Follow The Yellow Brick Road Collector Set
(set/5, LE-1999)
Issued: 1999 • To Be Closed: 1999
Original Price: $75
Value by Year Mark: **9**–$75

(5) #302716

Forever Yours,
Forever True
Issued: 1998 • Current
Original Price: $30
Value by Year Mark:
7–$30 **8**–$30 **9**–$30

FIGURINES

	Price Paid	Value Of My Collection
1.		
2.		
3.		
4.		
5.		
6.		
7.		

PENCIL TOTALS

(6) #352950

Frank and Helen
(1998 Catalog Exclusive)
Snow One Like You
Issued: 1998 • Closed: 1998
Original Price: $22.50
Value by Year Mark: **8**–$43

(7) #911747

Freda and Tina
Our Friendship Is A Perfect Blend
Issued: 1993 • Current
Original Price: $35
Value by Year Mark:
3–$72 **4**–$64 **5**–$54 **6**–$45
7–$38 **8**–$35 **9**–$35

FIGURINES

① #103772

Gail
*Catching The First Blossoms
Of Friendship*
Issued: 1995
Suspended: 1995 • Retired: 1998
Original Price: $20
Value by Year Mark:
5–$42 **6**–$33 **7**–$25 **8**–$22

② #912786

Gary
Truest Friendships Are Scarce
Issued: 1993 • Suspended: 1996
Original Price: $18.50
Value by Year Mark:
3–$52 **4**–$41 **5**–$33

③ #103640

Girl Cupid
Be Mine
Issued: 1995 • Suspended: 1995
Original Price: $15
Value by Year Mark: **4**–$34

④ #103640

Girl Cupid
Love
Issued: 1995 • Suspended: 1995
Original Price: $15
Value by Year Mark: **4**–$34

⑤ #477893

New!

Glenn (LE-1999)
*By Land Or By Sea, Let's Go –
Just You And Me*
Issued: 1999
To Be Closed: 1999
Original Price: $35
Value by Year Mark: **9**–$35

⑥ #163465

**Gordon
(International Exclusive)**
Keepin' A Watchful Eye On You
Issued: 1995 • Current
Original Price: N/A
Value by Year Mark:
5–$60 **6**–$42 **7**–$35
8–N/E **9**–N/E

⑦ #477907

New!

**Graduation
(1999 Avon Exclusive)**
*Always Put Your
Best Paw Forward*
Issued: 1999
To Be Closed: 1999
Original Price: $12.99
Value by Year Mark: **9**–$12.99

⑧ #912778

Gretel
We Make Magic, Me And You
Issued: 1993 • Retired: 1998
Original Price: $18.50
Value by Year Mark:
3–$52 **4**–$43 **5**–$36
6–$29 **7**–$24 **8**–$21

FIGURINES

	Price Paid	Value Of My Collection
1.		
2.		
3.		
4.		
5.		
6.		
7.		
8.		
PENCIL TOTALS		

① #302651

Growing Better Each Year
Issued: 1998 • Current
Original Price: $22.50
Value by Year Mark:
8–$22.50 **9**–$22.50

② #534145

New!

Haley and Logan
*Sisters And Hugs Soothe
The Soul*
Issued: 1999 • Current
Original Price: $25
Value by Year Mark:
8–$25 **9**–$25

③ #152382

Halloween House
Issued: 1995 • Current
Original Price: $20
Value: $20

④ #176206

**Halloween Mini Figurines
(set/3)**
Issued: 1996 • Current
Original Price: $15
Value: $15

⑤ #912956

Hans
Friends In Toyland
Issued: 1993
Suspended: 1995 • Retired: 1995
Original Price: $20
Value by Year Mark:
3–$138 **4**–$118

⑥ #911739

Harrison
We're Going Places
Issued: 1993 • Retired: 1997
Original Price: $15
Value by Year Mark:
3–$52 **4**–$43 **5**–$40 **6**–$33

FIGURINES

	Price Paid	Value Of My Collection
1.		
2.		
3.		
4.		
5.		
6.		
7.		
8.		

PENCIL TOTALS

⑦ #534129

New!

Hazel
*I've Got A Notion To Give
You A Potion*
Issued: 1999 • Current
Original Price: $15
Value by Year Mark:
8–$15 **9**–$15

⑧ #CRT240

**Heart To Heart
(1996 Event Exclusive)**
Issued: 1996 • Closed: 1996
Original Price: $12.50
Value: $30

FIGURINES

① #910708

Heidi and David
Special Friends
Issued: 1993 • Suspended: 1995
Original Price: $25
Value by Year Mark:
LETTER–$72 **3**–$59 **4**–$50

② #910686

Henrietta
A Basketful Of Wishes
Issued: 1993 • Suspended: 1994
Original Price: $22.50
Value by Year Mark:
LETTER–$185 **3**–$165

③ #916420

Henry
Celebrating Spring With You
Issued: 1994 • Suspended: 1995
Original Price: $20
Value by Year Mark:
3–$63 **4**–$52

④ #916285

Holding On To Someone Special
(1993 Customer Appreciation Exclusive)
Issued: 1993 • Closed: 1993
Original Price: $20
Value: $270

⑤ #534099

New!

Honey
You're A Good Friend That Sticks Like Honey
Issued: 1999 • Current
Original Price: $16.50
Value by Year Mark:
8–$16.50 **9**–$16.50

⑥ #103764

Hope
Our Love Is Ever-Blooming
Issued: 1995
Suspended: 1995 • Retired: 1998
Original Price: $20
Value by Year Mark:
4–$42 **5**–$37 **6**–$27
7–$23 **8**–$22

⑦ #352977

Humphrey
(1998 Event Exclusive)
Just The Bear Facts, Ma'am
Issued: 1998 • Closed: 1998
Original Price: $15
Value by Year Mark: **8**–$50

⑧ #354104

Hunter
Me Cave Bear, You Friend
Issued: 1998 • Retired: 1999
Original Price: $15
Value by Year Mark:
8–$26 **9**–$26

FIGURINES

	Price Paid	Value Of My Collection
1.		
2.		
3.		
4.		
5.		
6.		
7.		
8.		
PENCIL TOTALS		

① #302988

New!

If A Mom's Love Comes In All Sizes, Yours Has The Biggest Of Hearts (Gift To Go Exclusive, sold as set, #605344, w/mini figurine)
Issued: 1999
To Be Retired: 1999
Original Price: $25
Value by Year Mark: **9**–$25

② #617237

Ingrid (Dated 1994)
Bundled-up With Warm Wishes
Issued: 1994 • Closed: 1994
Original Price: $20
Value by Year Mark: **4**–$62

③ #476404

New!

Irene
Time Leads Us Back To The Things We Love The Most
Issued: 1999 • Current
Original Price: $20
Value by Year Mark:
8–$20 **9**–$20

④ #476943 ♣

New!

Irish Mini Figurines (2 asst.)
Good Luck
Issued: 1999 • Current
Original Price: $7.50
Value: $7.50

⑤ #476943 ♣

New!

Irish Mini Figurines (2 asst.)
Lucky Charm
Issued: 1999 • Current
Original Price: $7.50
Value: $7.50

⑥ #950432

Jacki
Hugs and Kisses
Issued: 1992 • Current
Original Price: $10
Value by Year Mark:
LETTER–$46 **3**–$40 **4**–$32 **5**–$23
6–$19 **7**–$13 **8**–$10 **9**–$10
Variation: no dots on hairbow, dots on heart, patch on arm
Value: $75

	FIGURINES	
	Price Paid	Value Of My Collection
1.		
2.		
3.		
4.		
5.		
6.		
7.		
8.		
	PENCIL TOTALS	

⑦ #950734

Jacob
Wishing For Love
Issued: 1992 • Suspended: 1996
Original Price: $22.50
Value by Year Mark:
LETTER–$67 **3**–$58 **4**–$48
5–$37 **6**–$33

⑧ #141224

Jamie and Ashley
I'm All Wrapped Up In Your Love
Issued: 1996 • Retired: 1998
Original Price: $25
Value by Year Mark:
6–$40 **7**–$32 **8**–$29

FIGURINES

#336521

Janet
(1998 Avon Exclusive)
You're Sweet As A Rose
Issued: 1998 • Closed: 1998
Original Price: $20
Value by Year Mark: **8**–$38

New!   #202940

Jasmine (GCC Exclusive)
A Bouquet Of Blessings For You
Issued: 1999
To Be Closed: 1999
Original Price: $15
Value by Year Mark: **9**–$15

#950475

Jasmine
You Have Touched My Heart
Issued: 1992 • Suspended: 1995
Original Price: $22.50
Value by Year Mark:
LETTER–$85 **3**–$73 **4**–$60

#269859

Jean (set/2)
Cup Full Of Peace
Issued: 1997 • Current
Original Price: $25
Value by Year Mark:
7–$28 **8**–$25 **9**–$25

#617091

Jedediah
Giving Thanks For Friends
Issued: 1994 • Retired: 1997
Original Price: $17.50
Value by Year Mark:
4–$52 **5**–$38 **6**–$33

#176044

Jeffrey (Dated 1996)
Striking Up Another Year
Issued: 1996 • Closed: 1996
Original Price: $17.50
Value by Year Mark: **6**–$25

#103810

Jennifer
Gathering The Blooms Of Friendship
Issued: 1995
Suspended: 1995 • Retired: 1998
Original Price: $22.50
Value by Year Mark:
4–$47 **5**–$40 **6**–$32
7–$28 **8**–$25

#950521

Jeremy
Friends Like You Are
Precious And True
Issued: 1992
Suspended: 1995 • Retired: 1995
Original Price: $15
Value by Year Mark:
LETTER–$90 **3**–$76 **4**–$70

	Price Paid	Value Of My Collection
1.		
2.		
3.		
4.		
5.		
6.		
7.		
8.		
FIGURINES		

PENCIL TOTALS

1 #546534
New!

Jerome
(1999 Avon Exclusive)
Can't Bear The Cold
Without You
Issued: 1999
To Be Closed: 1999
Original Price: $19.99
Value by Year Mark: **9**–$19.99

2 #155438

Jessica
A Mother's Heart Is Full Of Love
Issued: 1997 • Retired: 1997
Original Price: $25
Value by Year Mark:
6–$68 **7**–$53

3 #155438A

Jessica
(1996 Catalog Exclusive)
A Mother's Heart Is Full Of Love
Issued: 1996 • Closed: 1996
Original Price: $25
Value by Year Mark: **6**–$110

4 #269840

Joann (set/2)
Cup Full Of Love
Issued: 1997 • Current
Original Price: $25
Value by Year Mark:
7–$28 **8**–$25 **9**–$25

5 #476412
New!

Joe
Love Only Gets Better With Age
Issued: 1999 • Current
Original Price: $15
Value by Year Mark:
8–$15 **9**–$15

6 #533858
New!

John and William
When Friends Meet, Hearts Warm
Issued: 1999 • Current
Original Price: $35
Value by Year Mark:
8–$35 **9**–$35

FIGURINES

	Price Paid	Value Of My Collection
1.		
2.		
3.		
4.		
5.		
6.		
7.		
8.		
PENCIL TOTALS		

7 #911739

Jonathan
Sail With Me
Issued: 1993 • Retired: 1997
Original Price: $15
Value by Year Mark:
3–$51 **4**–$45 **5**–$38 **6**–$33

8 #269832

Jordan (set/2)
Cup Full Of Joy
Issued: 1997 • Current
Original Price: $25
Value by Year Mark:
7–$28 **8**–$25 **9**–$25

FIGURINES

① #476471

Joseph
*Everyone Has Their
"Old Friends" To Hug*
Issued: 1999 • Current
Original Price: $25
Value by Year Mark:
8–$25 **9**–$25

② #950556

Joshua
Love Repairs All
Issued: 1992 • Retired: 1997
Original Price: $20
Value by Year Mark:
LETTER–$58 **3**–$44 **4**–$40
5–$34 **6**–$28 **7**–$25

③ #534153

New!

June and Jean
*I've Always Wanted To
Be Just Like You*
Issued: 1999 • Current
Original Price: $20
Value by Year Mark:
8–$20 **9**–$20

④ #476641

New!

Junior
Everyone Is A Bear's Best Friend
Issued: 1999 • Current
Original Price: $12.50
Value by Year Mark:
8–$12.50 **9**–$12.50

⑤ #537810

New!

Justine and Janice
*Sisters And Friendship Are
Crafted With Love*
Issued: 1999 • Current
Original Price: $25
Value by Year Mark:
8–$25 **9**–$25

⑥ #265799

**Kara (1997 Adoption
Center Event Exclusive)**
You're A Honey Of A Friend
Issued: 1997 • Closed: 1997
Original Price: $15
Value by Year Mark: **7**–$37

⑦ #950432

Karen
Best Buddy
Issued: 1992 • Current
Original Price: $10
Value by Year Mark:
LETTER–$46 **3**–$40 **4**–$33 **5**–$24
6–$17 **7**–$14 **8**–$10 **9**–$10
*Variation: no dots on hairbow,
dots on heart, patch on arm*
Value by Year Mark: **4**–$90

⑧ #916447

Kathleen
Luck Found Me A Friend In You
Issued: 1994 • Current Δ
Original Price: $12.50
Value by Year Mark:
3–$33 **4**–$30 **5**–$25 **6**–$19
7–$15 **8**–$12.50 **9**–$12.50

FIGURINES	Price Paid	Value Of My Collection
1.		
2.		
3.		
4.		
5.		
6.		
7.	10.00	46.00
8.		
	10.00	46.00
PENCIL TOTALS		

① #950440

Katie
*A Friend Always Knows When
You Need A Hug*
Issued: 1992 • Retired: 1997
Original Price: $20
Value by Year Mark:
LETTER–$74 **3**–$60 **4**–$47
5–$42 **6**–$34

② New! #538299

③ New! #538299E

Katie, Renee, Jessica, Matthew
(1999 Event Exclusive)
I'm Surrounded By Hugs
Issued: 1999
To Be Closed: 1999
Original Price: $25
Value by Year Mark: **9**–$25

Katie, Renee, Jessica, Matthew
(1999 International Event Exclusive)
I'm Surrounded By Hugs
Issued: 1999
To Be Closed: 1999
Original Price: $25
Value by Year Mark: **9**–$25

④ New! #533815

Kayla
(1999 Event Exclusive)
*Big Hearts Come In
Small Packages*
Issued: 1999
To Be Closed: 1999
Original Price: $20
Value by Year Mark: **9**–$20

⑤ #354244

Keith and Deborah
The Holidays Are Twice As "Ice"
Issued: 1998 • Current
Original Price: $30
Value by Year Mark:
8–$30 **9**–$30

⑥ #916307

Kelly
You're My One And Only
Issued: 1994 • Suspended: 1995
Original Price: $15
Value by Year Mark:
3–$70 **4**–$60

	FIGURINES	
	Price Paid	Value Of My Collection
1.		
2.		
3.		
4.		
5.		
6.		
7.		
8.		
PENCIL TOTALS		

⑦ #103896

Kevin
Good Luck To You
Issued: 1995 • Retired: 1996
Original Price: $12.50
Value by Year Mark:
4–$48 **5**–$35 **6**–$32

⑧ #127965

Kiss The Hurt And Make It Well
Issued: 1995 • Current
Original Price: $15
Value by Year Mark:
4–$38 **5**–$32 **6**–$22
7–$17 **8**–$15 **9**–$15

FIGURINES

① #131865

Kittie (1996 Adoption Center Event Exclusive)
You Make Wishes Come True
Issued: 1996 • Closed: 1996
Original Price: $17.50
Value by Year Mark: **6**–$48

② #131865F

Kittie (1996 International Adoption Center Event Exclusive)
You Make Wishes Come True
Issued: 1996 • Closed: 1996
Original Price: N/A
Value by Year Mark: **6**–$58

③ #141194

Kristen
Hugs Of Love And Friendship
Issued: 1995 • Retired: 1998
Original Price: $20
Value by Year Mark:
5–$45 **6**–$32 **7**–$23 **8**–$22

④ #476390

New!

Kyle
Even Though We're Far Apart, You'll Always Have A Place In My Heart
Issued: 1999 • Current
Original Price: $15
Value by Year Mark:
8–$15 **9**–$15

⑤ #337463

Lance (1998 Event Exclusive)
Come Fly With Me
Issued: 1998 • Closed: 1998
Original Price: $20
Value by Year Mark: **8**–$28

⑥ #203440

Larry
You're My Shooting Star
Issued: 1997 • Current
Original Price: $17.50
Value by Year Mark:
7–$22 **8**–$17.50 **9**–$17.50

⑦ #156396

Laura
Friendship Makes It All Better
Issued: 1996 • Current
Original Price: $15
Value by Year Mark:
6–$26 **7**–$20 **8**–$15 **9**–$15

⑧ #272167

Lee (Dated 1997)
You're A Bear's Best Friend
Issued: 1997 • Closed: 1997
Original Price: $20
Value by Year Mark: **7**–$33

FIGURINES

	Price Paid	Value Of My Collection
1.		
2.		
3.		
4.		
5.		
6.		
7.	15.00	20.00
8.	20.00	33.00
	35.00	53.00
PENCIL TOTALS		

① #305979

Libby
My Country Tis Of Thee
Issued: 1998 • Retired: 1998
Original Price: $20
Value by Year Mark:
7–$35 **8**–$28

② #156426

Linda
*ABC And 1-2-3,
You're A Friend To Me!*
Issued: 1996 • Current
Original Price: $15
Value by Year Mark:
6–$23 **7**–$18 **8**–$15 **9**–$15

③ #103780

Lisa
My Best Is Always You
Issued: 1995
Suspended: 1995 • Retired: 1998
Original Price: $20
Value by Year Mark:
4–$46 **5**–$36 **6**–$30
7–$24 **8**–$22

④ #103659

Little Bundle Of Joy
Issued: 1995 • Suspended: 1995
Original Price: $13.50
Value by Year Mark: **4**–$32

⑤ #103659

Little Bundle Of Joy
Issued: 1995 • Suspended: 1995
Original Price: $13.50
Value by Year Mark: **4**–$32

⑥ #666963

New!

PHOTO UNAVAILABLE

**Loretta
(1999 Catalog Exclusive)**
Issued: 1999
To Be Closed: 1999
Original Price: $17.50
Value by Year Mark: **9**–$17.50

	FIGURINES	
	Price Paid	Value Of My Collection
1.		
2.		
3.		
4.		
5.		
6.		
7.		
8.		
PENCIL TOTALS		

⑦ #476439

New!

Lori
*Those We Love Should
Be Cherished*
Issued: 1999 • Current
Original Price: $17.50
Value by Year Mark:
8–$17.50 **9**–$17.50

⑧ #203432

Lou
Take Me Out To The Ball Game
Issued: 1998 • Current
Original Price: $15
Value by Year Mark:
7–$19 **8**–$15 **9**–$15

① #310735

Lynn
A Handmade Holiday Wish
Issued: 1998 • Current
Original Price: $25
Value by Year Mark:
8–$25 **9**–$25

② #310735A

Lynn
(1997 Catalog Exclusive)
A Handmade Holiday Wish
Issued: 1997 • Closed: 1997
Original Price: $25
Value by Year Mark: **7**–$42

③ #135593

Madeline
A Cup Full Of Friendship
Issued: 1995 • Retired: 1999
Original Price: $20
Value by Year Mark:
4–$36 **5**–$30 **6**–$24
7–$23 **8**–$22 **9**–$22

④ #950572

Mandy
I Love You Just The
Way You Are
Issued: 1992
Suspended: 1995 • Retired: 1995
Original Price: $15
Value by Year Mark:
LETTER–$83 **3**–$74 **4**–$62

⑤ #103667

Margaret
A Cup Full Of Love
Issued: 1995 • Retired: 1999
Original Price: $20
Value by Year Mark:
4–$36 **5**–$30 **6**–$24
7–$23 **8**–$22 **9**–$22

⑥ #475602

Margy
(1998 Avon Exclusive)
I'm Wrapping Up A Little
Holiday Joy To Send Your Way
Issued: 1998 • Closed: 1998
Original Price: $19.99
Value by Year Mark: **8**–N/E

⑦ #910767

Marie
Friendship Is A Special Treat
Issued: 1993 • Retired: 1999
Original Price: $20
Value by Year Mark:
LETTER–$60 **3**–$52 **4**–$46 **5**–$40
6–$28 **7**–$25 **8**–$22 **9**–$22
Variation: blue napkin,
white hearts on teapot
Value: $80

⑧ #135682

Marilyn
A Cup Full Of Cheer
Issued: 1995 • Retired: 1999
Original Price: $20
Value by Year Mark:
4–$34 **5**–$29 **6**–$24
7–$23 **8**–$22 **9**–$22

FIGURINES

	Price Paid	Value Of My Collection
1.		
2.		
3.		
4.		
5.		
6.		
7.		
8.		
PENCIL TOTALS		

FIGURINES

① #912840

Mary
A Special Friend Warms The Season
Issued: 1993 • Current
Original Price: $25
Value by Year Mark:
3–$58 **4**–$47 **5**–$40 **6**–$32
7–$27 **8**–$25 **9**–$25

② #476781

New!

Matt and Vicki (LE-1999)
*Love Is The Best Thing
Two Can Share*
Issued: 1999
To Be Closed: 1999
Original Price: $35
Value by Year Mark: **9**–$35

③ #135690

Maureen
Lucky Friend
Issued: 1995
Suspended: 1995 • Retired: 1996
Original Price: $12.50
Value by Year Mark:
4–$40 **5**–$35

④ #103829

Melissa
Every Bunny Needs A Friend
Issued: 1995
Suspended: 1995 • Retired: 1998
Original Price: $20
Value by Year Mark:
4–$43 **5**–$39 **6**–$27
7–$24 **8**–$22

⑤ #534226

New!

Meredith
*You're As Cozy As A
Pair Of Mittens!*
Issued: 1999 • Current
Original Price: $10
Value by Year Mark:
8–$10 **9**–$10

⑥ #910775

Michael and Michelle
Friendship Is A Cozy Feeling
Issued: 1993 • Suspended: 1995
Original Price: $30
Value by Year Mark:
LETTER–$84 **3**–$70 **4**–$60
Variation: yellow ruffle
Value: $97

FIGURINES

	Price Paid	Value Of My Collection
1.		
2.	35.00	35.00
3.		
4.		
5.		
6.		
7.		
8.		
	35.00	35.00

PENCIL TOTALS

⑦ #356255

**Mike (1998 Adoption
Center Event Exclusive)**
I'm Sweet On You
Issued: 1998 • Closed: 1998
Original Price: $15
Value by Year Mark: **8**–$33

⑧ #912751

Miles
*I'm Thankful For A
Friend Like You*
Issued: 1993 • Retired: 1998
Original Price: $17
Value by Year Mark:
3–$47 **4**–$38 **5**–$30 **6**–$24
7–$20 **8**–$19

① #128023

Millie
Love Me Tender
Issued: 1995 • Retired: 1996
Original Price: $12.50
Value by Year Mark:
4–$65 **5**–$48 **6**–$35
Variation: white ribbon with violet dots
Value by Year Mark: **5**–$68

② New! #534137

Milt and Garrett
A Haunting We Will Go
Issued: 1999 • Current
Original Price: $20
Value by Year Mark:
8–$20 **9**–$20

③ #156418

Mindy
*Friendship Keeps Me
On My Toes*
Issued: 1996 • Current
Original Price: $15
Value by Year Mark:
6–$26 **7**–$20 **8**–$15 **9**–$15

④ #910759

Molly
Friendship Softens A Bumpy Ride
Issued: 1993
Suspended: 1995 • Retired: 1996
Original Price: $30
Value by Year Mark:
LETTER–$85 **3**–$73 **4**–$65

⑤ #154016

**Mother Goose
And Friends**
Friends Of A Feather Flock Together
Issued: 1998 • Current
Original Price: $50
Value by Year Mark:
7–$57 **8**–$50 **9**–$50

⑥ New! #503711

**Mother's Day Mini
Figurines**
Grandma
Issued: 1999 • Current
Original Price: $7.50
Value: $7.50

⑦ New! #476773

**Mother's Day Mini
Figurines**
Mom
Issued: 1999 • Current
Original Price: $7.50
Value: $7.50

⑧ New! #503738

**Mother's Day Mini
Figurines**
Nana
Issued: 1999 • Current
Original Price: $7.50
Value: $7.50

FIGURINES

	Price Paid	Value Of My Collection
1.		
2.		
3.		
4.		
5.		
6.		
7.		
8.		
PENCIL TOTALS		

① #916315 ♥

Nancy
*Your Friendship Makes
My Heart Sing*
Issued: 1994
Suspended: 1995 • Retired: 1996
Original Price: $15
Value by Year Mark:
3–$112 **4**–$100

② New! #534110 🎃

Natalie
*You Make Me Smile
From Ear To Ear*
Issued: 1999 • Current
Original Price: $15
Value by Year Mark:
8–$15 **9**–$15

③ #176222 🦃

Nathan
Leave Your Worries Behind
Issued: 1998 • Current
Original Price: $17.50
Value by Year Mark:
8–$17.50 **9**–$17.50

④ #950513

Nathaniel and Nellie
It's Twice As Nice With You
Issued: 1992 • Retired: 1996
Original Price: $30
Value by Year Mark:
LETTER–$98 **3**–$78
4–$62 **5**–$56

⑤ #272361

Newton
*Ringing In The New Year
With Cheer*
Issued: 1997 • Current
Original Price: $15
Value by Year Mark:
7–$17 **8**–$15 **9**–$15

⑥ New! #534218 🎄

Nikki
*A Cold Winter's Day Won't
Keep Me Away*
Issued: 1999 • Current
Original Price: $10
Value by Year Mark:
8–$10 **9**–$10

FIGURINES

	Price Paid	Value Of My Collection
1.	15.00	112.00
2.		
3.		
4.		
5.		
6.		
7.		
	15.00	112.00

PENCIL TOTALS

⑦ #617245 🎄

Nils
Near And Deer For Christmas
Issued: 1994
Suspended: 1996 • Retired: 1997
Original Price: $22.50
Value by Year Mark:
4–$72 **5**–$58

FIGURINES

① #215864

Nina
(1997 Event Exclusive)
Beary Happy Wishes
Issued: 1997 • Closed: 1997
Original Price: $17.50
Value by Year Mark: **7**–$32

② New! #534188

Norbit and Nyla
(Dated 1999 & 2000)
*A Friend Is Someone Who
Reaches For Your Hand And
Touches Your Heart*
Issued: 1999
To Be Closed: 1999
Original Price: $25
Value by Year Mark: **9**–$25

③ New! #476765

Norm
Patience Is A Fisherman's Virtue
Issued: 1999 • Current
Original Price: $25
Value by Year Mark:
8–$25 **9**–$25

④ #182966

Olga (LE-1996)
*Feel The Peace ... Hold The
Joy ... Share The Love*
Issued: 1996 • Closed: 1996
Original Price: $50
Value by Year Mark: **6**–$75

⑤ #916641

Oliver & Olivia
Will You Be Mine
Issued: 1994 • Suspended: 1995
Original Price: $25
Value by Year Mark:
3–$85 **4**–$74

⑥ #141313

Pat
Falling For You
Issued: 1995 • Current
Original Price: $22.50
Value by Year Mark:
5–$44 **6**–$30 **7**–$25 **8**–$22.50
9–$22.50
Variation: blue shirt on doll
Value by Year Mark: **5**–$48

⑦ #617105

Patience
Happiness Is Homemade
Issued: 1994 • Retired: 1997
Original Price: $17.50
Value by Year Mark:
4–$52 **5**–$38 **6**–$32

FIGURINES		
	Price Paid	Value Of My Collection
1.		
2.		
3.		
4.		
5.		
6.		
7.		
PENCIL TOTALS		

FIGURINES

① #911429

Patrice
Thank You For The Sky So Blue
Issued: 1993 • Retired: 1999
Original Price: $18.50
Value by Year Mark:
LETTER–$60 **3**–$50 **4**–$42 **5**–$36
6–$26 **7**–$24 **8**–$22 **9**–$22
Variation: bunny with white tail
Value : $44

② #911410

Patrick
*Thank You For A Friend
That's True*
Issued: 1993 • Retired: 1999
Original Price: $18.50
Value by Year Mark:
LETTER–$62 **3**–$50 **4**–$42 **5**–$36
6–$26 **7**–$24 **8**–$22 **9**–$22

③ New! #466328

Paul
**(1999 Adoption Center
Exclusive, LE-35,000)**
*Good Friends Warm The Heart
With Many Blessings*
Issued: 1999
To Be Closed: 1999
Original Price: $22.50
Value by Year Mark: **9**–$22.50

④ New! #466328I

Paul
**(1999 International
Adoption Center
Exclusive, LE-20,000)**
*Good Friends Warm The Heart
With Many Blessings*
Issued: 1999
To Be Closed: 1999
Original Price: $22.50
Value by Year Mark: **9**–$22.50

⑤ #337579

Penny, Chandler, Boots
**(1998 Adoption Center
Exclusive, LE-25,000)**
We're Inseparable
Issued: 1998 • Closed: 1998
Original Price: $25
Value by Year Mark: **8**–$50

⑥ #337579F

Penny, Chandler, Boots
**(1998 International
Adoption Center
Exclusive, LE-20,000)**
We're Inseparable
Issued: 1998 • Closed: 1998
Original Price: N/A
Value by Year Mark: **8**–$52

FIGURINES

	Price Paid	Value Of My Collection
1.		
2.		
3.		
4.		
5.		
6.		
7.	17.50	45.00
8.		
	17.50	45.00

PENCIL TOTALS

⑦ #104973

Peter
You're Some Bunny Special
Issued: 1995
Suspended: 1995 • Retired: 1998
Original Price: $17.50
Value by Year Mark:
4–$45 **5**–$39 **6**–$27
7–$24 **8**–$21
Variation: darker eggs, narrow base
Value: $50

⑧ #617113

Phoebe
*A Little Friendship Is
A Big Blessing*
Issued: 1994 • Retired: 1995
Original Price: $13.50
Value by Year Mark:
4–$68 **5**–$59

FIGURINES

1 #910724

Priscilla
Love Surrounds Our Friendship
Issued: 1993 • Retired: 1997
Original Price: $15
Value by Year Mark:
LETTER–$75 **3**–$60 **4**–$47
5–$36 **6**–$30

2 #128031

**Priscilla & Greta
(set/2, LE-19,950)**
Our Hearts Belong To You
Issued: 1995 • Closed: 1996
Original Price: $50
Value: $125

3 #128031F

**Priscilla & Greta
(International Exclusive,
LE-10,000)**
Our Hearts Belong To You
Issued: 1995 • Closed: 1995
Original Price: N/A
Value: $150

4 #CRT025

**Priscilla Ann
(1994-95 Expo Exclusive)**
There's No One Like Hue
Issued: 1994 • Closed: 1995
Original Price: $25
Value by Year Mark: **4**–$260

5 #912808

Prudence
A Friend To Be Thankful For
Issued: 1993 • Retired: 1998
Original Price: $17
Value by Year Mark:
3–$52 **4**–$40 **5**–$29
6–$25 **7**–$22 **8**–$20

6 #476498 New!

Randy
*You're Never Alone With
Good Friends Around*
Issued: 1999 • Current
Original Price: $22.50
Value by Year Mark:
8–$22.50 **9**–$22.50

7 #269999

Rex
*Our Friendship Will
Never Be Extinct*
Issued: 1997 • Current
Original Price: $17.50
Value by Year Mark:
7–$20 **8**–$17.50 **9**–$17.50

8 #352721

Rich (Dated 1998)
Always Paws For Holiday Treats
Issued: 1998 • Closed: 1998
Original Price: $22.50
Value by Year Mark: **8**–$30

FIGURINES

	Price Paid	Value Of My Collection
1.		
2.		
3.		
4.		
5.		
6.		
7.		
8.	22.50	30.00
	22.50	30.00
PENCIL TOTALS		

① New! #476617

Rita
(NALED Exclusive)
*Wishing You Love Straight
From The Heart*
Issued: 1999
To Be Closed: 1999
Original Price: $17.50
Value by Year Mark: **9**–$17.50

② #911402

Robbie and Rachel
Love Bears All Things
Issued: 1993 • Current
Original Price: $27.50
Value by Year Mark:
3–$63 **4**–$52 **5**–$42 **6**–$35
7–$32 **8**–$30 **9**–$30

③ #156272

Robert
Love Keeps Me Afloat
Issued: 1996 • Retired: 1999
Original Price: $13.50
Value by Year Mark:
5–$42 **6**–$30 **7**–$18
8–$13.50 **9**–$13.50

④ New! #533882

Rodney
(Gift To Go Exclusive,
sold as set, #646504,
w/plush piece)
I'm Santa's Little Helper
Issued: 1999
To Be Retired: 1999
Original Price: $25
Value by Year Mark: **9**–$25

⑤ New! #601586

Roxie & Shelly
What A Story We Share!
Issued: 1999 • Current
Original Price: $25
Value by Year Mark:
8–$25 **9**–$25

⑥ #466298

Roy
(1998 Event Exclusive)
I'm Your Country Cowboy
Issued: 1998 • Closed: 1998
Original Price: $17.50
Value by Year Mark: **8**–$28

FIGURINES		
	Price Paid	Value Of My Collection
1.		
2.		
3.		
4.		
5.		
6.		
7.		
8.		
PENCIL TOTALS		

⑦ New! #476668

Ruth & Gene
*Even When We Don't See
Eye To Eye, We're Always
Heart To Heart*
Issued: 1999 • Current
Original Price: $25
Value by Year Mark:
8–$25 **9**–$25

⑧ #203041

Ryan
I'm Green With Envy For You
Issued: 1997 • Current
Original Price: $20
Value by Year Mark:
6–$29 **7**–$24 **8**–$20 **9**–$20

FIGURINES

① #510955

New!

Sally & Skip
(1999 Adoption Center
Exclusive, LE-25,000)
We Make A Perfect Team
Issued: 1999
To Be Closed: 1999
Original Price: $27.50
Value by Year Mark: **9**–$27.50

② #510955F

New!

Sally & Skip
(1999 International
Adoption Center
Exclusive, LE-20,000)
We Make A Perfect Team
Issued: 1999
To Be Closed: 1999
Original Price: $27.50
Value by Year Mark: **9**–$27.50

③ #302619

Sam
I Want You ... To Be My Friend
Issued: 1998 • Retired: 1998
Original Price: $17.50
Value by Year Mark:
7–$35 **8**–$28

④ #950432

Sara
Love Ya
Issued: 1992 • Current
Original Price: $10
Value by Year Mark:
LETTER–$53 **3**–$40 **4**–$32 **5**–$26
6–$22 **7**–$14 **8**–$10 **9**–$10
Variation: no dots on hairbow,
dots on heart, patch on arm
Value by Year Mark: **4**–$100

⑤ #916439

Sean
Luck Found Me A Friend In You
Issued: 1994 • Current Δ
Original Price: $12.50
Value by Year Mark:
3–$42 **4**–$35 **5**–$25 **6**–$20
7–$15 **8**–$12.50 **9**–$12.50

⑥ #534102

New!

Sedley
We've Turned Over A New Leaf
On Our Friendship
Issued: 1999 • Current
Original Price: $16.50
Value by Year Mark:
8–$16.50 **9**–$16.50

⑦ #352799

Segrid, Justaf & Ingmar
(LE-1998)
The Spirit Of Christmas
Grows In Our Hearts
Issued: 1998 • Closed: 1998
Original Price: $45
Value by Year Mark: **8**–$55

FIGURINES

	Price Paid	Value Of My Collection
1.		
2.		
3.		
4.		
5.		
6.		
7.	45.00	55.00
	45.00	55.00
PENCIL TOTALS		

67

① #103551

Sent With Love
Issued: 1995 • Suspended: 1995
Original Price: $17.50
Value by Year Mark: **4**–$40

② #128015

Seth and Sarabeth
We're Beary Good Pals
Issued: 1995 • Retired: 1999
Original Price: $25
Value by Year Mark:
4–$50 **5**–$42 **6**–$32
7–$30 **8**–$27 **9**–$27

③ #354260

Shannon
*A Figure 8,
Our Friendship Is Great!*
Issued: 1998 • Current
Original Price: $20
Value by Year Mark:
8–$20 **9**–$20

④ #163481

**Sherlock
(International Exclusive)**
Good Friends Are Hard To Find
Issued 1995 • Current
Original Price: N / A
Value by Year Mark:
5–$64 **6**–$44 **7**–$35
8–N / E **9**–N / E

⑤ #466271

**Sierra
(1998 Event Exclusive)**
You're My Partner
Issued: 1998 • Closed: 1998
Original Price: $17.50
Value by Year Mark: **8**–$28

⑥ #601551

New!

Simone & Jhodi
I've Always Believed In You
Issued: 1999 • Current
Original Price: $25
Value by Year Mark:
8–$25 **9**–$25

FIGURINES

	Price Paid	Value Of My Collection
1.		
2.		
3.		
4.		
5.		
6.		
7.		
8.		

PENCIL TOTALS

⑦ #302643

**Sixteen Candles And
Many More Wishes**
Issued: 1998 • Current
Original Price: $22.50
Value by Year Mark:
7–$22.50 **8**–$22.50 **9**–$22.50

⑧ #601594

New!

Skylar & Shana
*When You Find A Sunbeam,
Share The Warmth*
Issued: 1999 • Current
Original Price: $25
Value by Year Mark:
8–$25 **9**–$25

FIGURINES

---

① #622818

Sonja
Holiday Cuddles
Issued: 1994 • Retired: 1998
Original Price: $20
Value by Year Mark:
4–$46 **5**–$36 **6**–$27
7–$23 **8**–$22

---

② #916358

**Spring Mini Figurines
(3 asst.)**
Girl With Blue Bonnet And Duck
Issued: 1994 • Current
Original Price: $7
Value: $7

---

③ #916358

**Spring Mini Figurines
(3 asst.)**
Girl With Daisy Headband
Issued: 1994 • Current
Original Price: $7
Value: $7

---

④ #916358

**Spring Mini Figurines
(3 asst.)**
Girl With White Hat And Flower
Issued: 1994 • Current
Original Price: $7
Value: $7

---

⑤ #617148

Stacie
You Lift My Spirit
Issued: 1994 • Retired: 1998
Original Price: $18.50
Value by Year Mark:
4–$50 **5**–$42 **6**–$30
7–$28 **8**–$24

---

⑥ #476676

New!

**Stanley & Valerie
(covered box)**
*Togetherness Is The Reason
We Have Friends*
Issued: 1999 • Current
Original Price: $35
Value by Year Mark:
8–$35 **9**–$35

---

⑦ #534250

New!

Star (LE-1999)
*Cherish Yesterday, Dream
Tomorrow, Live Today*
Issued: 1999
To Be Closed: 1999
Original Price: $55
Value by Year Mark: **9**–$55

---

⑧ #951129

Steven
A Season Filled With Sweetness
Issued: 1992 • Retired: 1995
Original Price: $20
Value by Year Mark:
LETTER–$88 **3**–$73 **4**–$66 **5**–$57

FIGURINES

	Price Paid	Value Of My Collection
1.		
2.		
3.		
4.		
5.		
6.		
7.		
8.		
PENCIL TOTALS		

① #272159

Sven and Liv (LE-1997)
*All Paths Lead To Kindness
And Friendship*
Issued: 1997 • Closed: 1997
Original Price: $55
Value by Year Mark: **7**–$75

② #265810

**Sylvia
(1997 Event Exclusive)**
A Picture Perfect Friendship
Issued: 1997 • Closed: 1997
Original Price: $15
Value by Year Mark: **7**–$77

③ #176257

Tabitha
You're The Cat's Meow
Issued: 1996 • Retired: 1998
Original Price: $15
Value by Year Mark:
6–$28 **7**–$20 **8**–$18

④ #510947

New!

**Tammy
(1999 Event Exclusive)**
Let's Go To The Hop!
Issued: 1999
To Be Closed: 1999
Original Price: $15
Value by Year Mark: **9**–$15

⑤ #156353

**Tasha
(1996 Adoption Center
Exclusive, LE-19,960)**
In Grandmother's Attic
Issued: 1996 • Closed: 1996
Original Price: $55
Value by Year Mark: **6**–$165

⑥ #156353F

**Tasha
(1996 International
Adoption Center
Exclusive, LE-10,000)**
In Grandmother's Attic
Issued: 1996 • Closed: 1996
Original Price: N/A
Value: $220

FIGURINES

	Price Paid	Value Of My Collection
1.		
2.		
3.		
4.		
5.		
6.		
7.	15.00	45.00
8.		
	15.00	45.00

PENCIL TOTALS

⑦ #617156

Taylor
Sail The Seas With Me
Issued: 1994 • Suspended: 1996
Original Price: $15
Value by Year Mark:
4–$52 **5**–$45

⑧ #476757

New!

Teddy
Friends Give You Wings To Fly
Issued: 1999 • Current
Original Price: $15
Value by Year Mark:
8–$15 **9**–$15

FIGURINES

① #624918

**Teddy and Roosevelt
(LE-1993)**
The Book Of Teddies 1903-1993
Issued: 1993 • Closed: 1993
Original Price: $20
Value by Year Mark: **3**–$215

② #617075

Thanksgiving Quilt
Issued: 1994 • Current
Original Price: $12
Value: $12

③ #912883

**Theadore, Samantha
and Tyler (9")**
Friendship Weathers All Storms
Issued: 1993 • Suspended: 1995
Original Price: $160
Value by Year Mark:
3–$225 **4**–$200

④ #950505

**Theadore, Samantha
and Tyler**
Friends Come In All Sizes
Issued: 1992 • Current
Original Price: $20
Value by Year Mark:
LETTER–$89 **3**–$58 **4**–$46 **5**–$37
6–$28 **7**–$23 **8**–$20 **9**–$20
*Variation: Theadore with blue
heart patch*
Value by Year Mark: **4**–$120

⑤ #950769

**Theadore, Samantha
and Tyler**
Friendship Weathers All Storms
Issued: 1992 • Retired: 1997
Original Price: $17
Value by Year Mark:
LETTER–$100 **3**–$80 **4**–$72
5–$58 **6**–$45

⑥ #951196

**Theadore, Samantha
and Tyler (9")**
Friends Come In All Sizes
Issued: 1992 • Current
Original Price: $130
Value by Year Mark:
LETTER–$175 **3**–$155 **4**–$147
5–$138 **6**–$135
7–$132 **8**–$130 **9**–$130

⑦ #215910

**This Calls For A
Celebration**
Issued: 1997 • Current
Original Price: $15
Value by Year Mark:
7–$15 **8**–$15 **9**–$15

	Price Paid	Value Of My Collection
FIGURINES		
1.		
2.		
3.		
4.		
5.		
6.		
7.		
PENCIL TOTALS		

① #911739

Thomas
Chuggin' Along
Issued: 1993 • Retired: 1997
Original Price: $15
Value by Year Mark:
3–$58 **4**–$50 **5**–$38 **6**–$33

② #910740

Timothy
A Friend Is Forever
Issued: 1993
Suspended: 1995 • Retired: 1996
Original Price: $15
Value by Year Mark:
LETTER–$75 **3**–$62 **4**–$50

③ #911372

Tracie and Nicole
Side By Side With Friends
Issued: 1993 • Retired: 1999
Original Price: $35
Value by Year Mark:
3–$72 **4**–$60 **5**–$54 **6**–$45
7–$40 **8**–$38 **9**–$38

④ #354112

Trevor
You Bring Out The Devil In Me
Issued: 1998 • Current
Original Price: $17.50
Value by Year Mark:
8–$17.50 **9**–$17.50

⑤ #127973

Tucker & Travis
We're In This Together
Issued: 1995 • Current
Original Price: $25
Value by Year Mark:
4–$47 **5**–$38 **6**–$32
7–$27 **8**–$25 **9**–$25

⑥ #916382

**Valentine Mini Figurines
(3 asst.)**
Hugs & Kisses
Issued: 1994
Out Of Production: 1998
Original Price: $7
Value: $9

FIGURINES

	Price Paid	Value Of My Collection
1.		
2.		
3.		
4.		
5.		
6.		
7.		
8.		
PENCIL TOTALS		

⑦ #916382

**Valentine Mini Figurines
(3 asst.)**
Love Ya
Issued: 1994
Out Of Production: 1998
Original Price: $7
Value: $9

⑧ #916382

**Valentine Mini Figurines
(3 asst.)**
You're Purr-fect
Issued: 1994
Out Of Production: 1998
Original Price: $7
Value: $9

FIGURINES

① #366854

Veronica
(1998 Catalog Exclusive)
You Make Happiness Bloom
Issued: 1998 • Closed: 1998
Original Price: $15
Value by Year Mark: **8**–$38

② #916293

Victoria
From My Heart To Yours
Issued: 1994 • Suspended: 1995
Original Price: $16.50
Value by Year Mark:
3–$115 **4**–$100 **5**–$85

③ #156280

Violet
Blessings Bloom When
You Are Near
Issued: 1996 • Retired: 1999
Original Price: $15
Value by Year Mark:
5–$30 **6**–$24 **7**–$20
8–$17 **9**–$17

④ #302678

Whitney
We Make A Winning Team
Issued: 1998 • Current
Original Price: $15
Value by Year Mark:
7–$17 **8**–$15 **9**–$15

⑤ #617164

Willie
Bears Of A Feather Stay Together
Issued: 1994 • Retired: 1997
Original Price: $15
Value by Year Mark:
4–$57 **5**–$49 **6**–$38

⑥ New! #476811

Winfield
(Special Millennium
Limited Edition)
Anything Is Possible When
You Wish On A Star
Issued: 1999 • Current
Original Price: $50
Value by Year Mark:
8–$50 **9**–$50

⑦ #617172

Winona
Little Fair Feather Friend
Issued: 1994 • Retired: 1997
Original Price: $15
Value by Year Mark:
4–$55 **5**–$48 **6**–$38

⑧ #629707

Wyatt
I'm Called Little Running Bear
Issued: 1994 • Retired: 1998
Original Price: $15
Value by Year Mark:
4–$46 **5**–$38 **6**–$29
7–$25 **8**–$22

	Price Paid	Value Of My Collection
FIGURINES		
1.		
2.		
3.		
4.		
5.		
6.		
7.		
8.		
PENCIL TOTALS		

① #617121

Wylie
I'm Called Little Friend
Issued: 1994 • Retired: 1998
Original Price: $15
Value by Year Mark:
4–$48 **5**–$38 **6**–$30
7–$25 **8**–$22

② #215880

You Grow More Dear With Each Passing Year
Issued: 1997 • Current
Original Price: $25
Value by Year Mark:
7–$25 **8**–$25 **9**–$25

③ #306398

You're The Frosting On The Birthday Cake
Issued: 1998 • Current
Original Price: $22.50
Value by Year Mark:
7–$22.50 **8**–$22.50 **9**–$22.50

④ #302759

You're The Key To My Heart Mini Figurine
Issued: 1998 • Current
Original Price: $7.50
Value: $7.50

⑤ #302759

You're The Key To My Heart Mini Figurine
Issued: 1998 • Current
Original Price: $7.50
Value: $7.50

⑥ #950491

Zachary
Yesterday's Memories Are Today's Treasures
Issued: 1992 • Retired: 1997
Original Price: $30
Value by Year Mark:
LETTER–$84 **3**–$70 **4**–$58
5–$52 **6**–$45

FIGURINES		
	Price Paid	Value Of My Collection
1.		
2.		
3.		
4.		
5.		
6.	30.00	58.00
	30.00	58.00
PENCIL TOTALS		

SERIES

Many **Cherished Teddies** pieces are released as members of series. A collector can accumulate teddies with an international theme from those in the *Across The Seas* series, decorate for the summer with pieces from *By The Sea, By The Sea* series or make an extensive holiday display with teddies from the *Nativity* series, the *Nutcracker Suite* series and the *Santa* series. The new series for 1999 include *Antique Toy, Baby's 1st Christmas, Beary-Go-Round Carousels, Let Heaven And Nature Sing, Old Fashioned Country Christmas, Our Cherished Day, School Days, Teddie Triumphs* and *Teddies In Motion.*

Across The Seas

ACROSS THE SEAS *(side tab)*

---

① #276995

Bazza (Australia)
I'm Lost Down Under Without You
Issued: 1997 • Current
Original Price: $17.50
Value by Year Mark:
7–$17.50 **8**–$17.50 **9**–$17.50

② #276995P

Bazza (International Exclusive)
I'm Lost Down Under Without You
Issued: 1996 • Current
Original Price: N/A
Value by Year Mark: N/E

---

③ #202444P

Bob (United States, w/U.S. Passport)
Our Friendship Is From Sea To Shining Sea
Issued: 1996 • Current
Original Price: $17.50
Value by Year Mark:
6–$28 **7**–$17.50
8–$17.50 **9**–$17.50

④ #202339

Carlos (Mexico)
I Found An Amigo In You
Issued: 1996 • Current
Original Price: $17.50
Value by Year Mark:
6–$28 **7**–$17.50
8–$17.50 **9**–$17.50

ACROSS THE SEAS		
	Price Paid	Value Of My Collection
1.		
2.		
3.		
4.		
PENCIL TOTALS		

(1) #197254

Claudette (France)
Our Friendship Is Bon Appetit!
Issued: 1996 • Current
Original Price: $17.50
Value by Year Mark:
6–$28 **7**–$17.50
8–$17.50 **9**–$17.50

(2) #373966

Colleen (Ireland)
The Luck Of The Irish To You
Issued: 1998 • Current
Original Price: $17.50
Value by Year Mark:
8–$17.50 **9**–$17.50

(3) #202355

Fernando (Spain)
You Make Everyday A Fiesta
Issued: 1996 • Current
Original Price: $17.50
Value by Year Mark:
6–$28 **7**–$17.50
8–$17.50 **9**–$17.50

(4) #202436

Franz (Germany)
*Our Friendship Knows
No Boundaries*
Issued: 1996 • Current
Original Price: $17.50
Value by Year Mark:
6–$28 **7**–$17.50
8–$17.50 **9**–$17.50

(5) #202436P

**Franz
(International Exclusive)**
*Our Friendship Knows
No Boundaries*
Issued: 1996 • Current
Original Price: N/A
Value by Year Mark: N/E

(6) #202401

Katrien (Holland)
Tulips Blossom With Friendship
Issued: 1996 • Current
Original Price: $17.50
Value by Year Mark:
6–$28 **7**–$17.50
8–$17.50 **9**–$17.50
*Variation: "Cherished" missing
on bottom*
Value by Year Mark: **6**–$45

ACROSS THE SEAS

	Price Paid	Value Of My Collection
1.		
2.		
3.		
4.		
5.		
6.		
7.		
8.		

PENCIL TOTALS

(7) #202401P

**Katrien
(International Exclusive)**
Tulips Blossom With Friendship
Issued: 1996 • Current
Original Price: N/A
Value by Year Mark: N/E

(8) #197289

Kerstin (Sweden)
You're The Swedish Of Them All
Issued: 1996 • Current
Original Price: $17.50
Value by Year Mark:
6–$28 **7**–$17.50
8–$17.50 **9**–$17.50

ACROSS THE SEAS

① #302627

Leilani (Tahiti)
Sending You Warm And Friendly Island Breezes
Issued: 1998 • Retired: 1998
Original Price: $17.50
Value by Year Mark: **8**–$26

② #202347

Lian (China)
Our Friendship Spans Many Miles
Issued: 1996 • Retired: 1998
Original Price: $17.50
Value by Year Mark:
6–$28 **7**–$22 **8**–$20

③ #202452

Lorna (Scotland)
Our Love Is In The Highlands
Issued: 1996 • Current
Original Price: $17.50
Value by Year Mark:
6–$28 **7**–$17.50
8–$17.50 **9**–$17.50

④ #202452P

**Lorna
(International Exclusive)**
Our Love Is In The Highlands
Issued: 1996 • Current
Original Price: N/A
Value by Year Mark: N/E

⑤ #202312

Machiko (Japan)
Love Fans A Beautiful Friendship
Issued: 1996 • Retired: 1998
Original Price: $17.50
Value by Year Mark:
6–$28 **7**–$22 **8**–$20

⑥ #202320

Nadia (Russia)
From Russia, With Love
Issued: 1996 • Current
Original Price: $17.50
Value by Year Mark:
6–$28 **7**–$17.50
8–$17.50 **9**–$17.50

⑦ #216739

Preston (Canada)
Riding Across The Great White North
Issued: 1996 • Retired: 1998
Original Price: $17.50
Value by Year Mark:
6–$28 **7**–$22 **8**–$20

⑧ #216739P

**Preston
(International Exclusive)**
Riding Across The Great White North
Issued: 1996 • Current
Original Price: N/A
Value by Year Mark: N/E

ACROSS THE SEAS

	Price Paid	Value Of My Collection
1.		
2.		
3.		
4.		
5.		
6.		
7.		
8.		
	PENCIL TOTALS	

(1) #202398

Rajul (India)
You're The Jewel Of My Heart
Issued: 1996 • Current
Original Price: $17.50
Value by Year Mark:
6–$28 **7**–$17.50
8–$17.50 **9**–$17.50

(2) #276987

Sophia (Italy)
Like Grapes On The Vine, Our Friendship Is Divine
Issued: 1997 • Current
Original Price: $17.50
Value by Year Mark:
7–$17.50 **8**–$17.50 **9**–$17.50

(3) #202878

William (England)
You're A Jolly Ol' Chap!
Issued: 1996 • Current
Original Price: $17.50
Value by Year Mark:
6–$28 **7**–$17.50
8–$17.50 **9**–$17.50

(4) #202878P

**William
(International Exclusive)**
You're A Jolly Ol' Chap!
Issued: 1996 • Current
Original Price: N/A
Value by Year Mark: N/E

Angels

(5) #175986

Angela (LE-1998)
Peace On Earth And Mercy Mild
Issued: 1998 • Closed: 1998
Original Price: $20
Value by Year Mark: **8**–$33

ACROSS THE SEAS

	Price Paid	Value Of My Collection
1.		
2.		
3.		
4.		

ANGELS

5.		
6.		
7.		

PENCIL TOTALS

(6) #175994

Grace (LE-1997)
Glory To The Newborn King
Issued: 1997 • Closed: 1997
Original Price: $20
Value by Year Mark: **7**–$40

(7) #176001

Stormi (LE-1996)
Hark The Herald Angels Sing
Issued: 1996 • Closed: 1996
Original Price: $20
Value by Year Mark: **6**–$48

Antique Toy

① New! #537217

A Big Hug From A Little Friend
Issued: 1999 • Current
Original Price: $12.50
Value: $12.50

② New! #537187

Everyone Needs An Occasional Hug
Issued: 1999 • Current
Original Price: $12.50
Value: $12.50

③ New! #537241

Follow Your Heart Wherever It Takes You
Issued: 1999 • Current
Original Price: $12.50
Value: $12.50

④ New! #537233

A Friend Is An Answered Prayer
Issued: 1999 • Current
Original Price: $12.50
Value: $12.50

⑤ New! #537268

A Journey With You Is One To Remember
Issued: 1999 • Current
Original Price: $12.50
Value: $12.50

⑥ New! #537195

Keep Good Friends Close To Your Heart
Issued: 1999 • Current
Original Price: $12.50
Value: $12.50

⑦ New! #537209

Our Friendship Is An Adventure
Issued: 1999 • Current
Original Price: $12.50
Value: $12.50

ANTIQUE TOY		
	Price Paid	Value Of My Collection
1.		
2.		
3.		
4.		
5.		
6.		
7.		
PENCIL TOTALS		

1 #537225

New!

You Have The Biggest Heart Of All
Issued: 1999 • Current
Original Price: $12.50
Value: $12.50

Baby's 1st Christmas

2 #533327

New!

Baby's 1st Christmas Cross
Issued: 1999 • Current
Original Price: $17.50
Value: $17.50

3 #536938

New!

Baby's 1st Christmas Musical
♪ *Hush Little Baby*
Issued: 1999 • Current
Original Price: $40
Value: $40

4 #536911

New!

Baby's 1st Christmas Nightlight
Issued: 1999 • Current
Original Price: $40
Value: $40

5 #533300

New!

Baby's 1st Christmas Photo Frame Ornament
Issued: 1999 • Current
Original Price: $15
Value: $15

ANTIQUE TOY

	Price Paid	Value Of My Collection
1.		

BABY'S 1ST CHRISTMAS

2.		
3.		
4.		
5.		
6.		
7.		

PENCIL TOTALS

6 #533343

New!

Baby's 1st Christmas Rattle Ornament
Issued: 1999 • Current
Original Price: $15
Value: $15

7 #533335

New!

Baby's 1st Christmas Spoon Ornament
Issued: 1999 • Current
Original Price: $12.50
Value: $12.50

① **New!** #533297

Bianca
Sweet Dreams My Little One
Issued: 1999 • Current
Original Price: $15
Values by Year Mark:
8–$15 **9**–$15

Beary-Go-Round Carousel

② **New!** #589977

Archie
*Through Ups And
Downs, You're Still The Best
Friend Around*
Issued: 1999 • Current
Original Price: $20
Value by Year Mark:
8–$20 **9**–$20

③ **New!** #505552

Bill
*Friends Like You Are
Always True Blue*
Issued: 1999 • Current
Original Price: $20
Value by Year Mark:
8–$20 **9**–$20

④ **New!** #505498

Cody
*I'll Cherish You For
Many Moons*
Issued: 1999 • Current
Original Price: $20
Value by Year Mark:
8–$20 **9**–$20

⑤ **New!** #589942

Crystal
*Hang On!
We're In For A Wonderful Ride*
Issued: 1999 • Current
Original Price: $20
Value by Year Mark:
8–$20 **9**–$20

⑥ **New!** #589942R

Crystal (Rare Bear)
*Hang On!
We're In For A Wonderful Ride*
Issued: 1999
To Be Closed: 1999
Original Price: $20
Value by Year Mark: **9**–$20

⑦ **New!** #589950

Flossie
*I'd Stick My Neck Out
For You Anytime*
Issued: 1999 • Current
Original Price: $20
Value by Year Mark:
8–$20 **9**–$20

BABY'S 1ST CHRISTMAS

	Price Paid	Value Of My Collection
1.		

BEARY-GO-ROUND CAROUSEL

2.		
3.		
4.		
5.		
6.		
7.		
PENCIL TOTALS		

① New! #502898

Gina
Where Friends Gather,
Magic Blossoms
Issued: 1999 • Current
Original Price: $20
Value by Year Mark:
8–$20 **9**–$20

② New! #589969

Ivan
I've Packed My Trunk And
I'm Ready To Go
Issued: 1999 • Current
Original Price: $20
Value by Year Mark:
8–$20 **9**–$20

③ New! #506214

Jason
When It Comes To Friendship,
You've Really Earned
Your Stripes
Issued: 1999 • Current
Original Price: $20
Value by Year Mark:
8–$20 **9**–$20

④ New! #505579

Jenelle
A Friend Is Somebunny To
Cherish Forever
Issued: 1999 • Current
Original Price: $20
Value by Year Mark:
8–$20 **9**–$20

⑤ New! #589926

Jerrod
Don't Worry – It's Just Another
Little Bump In The Road
Issued: 1999 • Current
Original Price: $20
Value by Year Mark:
8–$20 **9**–$20

⑥ New! #589934

Marcus
There's Nobody I'd Rather Go
'Round With Than You
Issued: 1999 • Current
Original Price: $20
Value by Year Mark:
8–$20 **9**–$20

BEARY-GO-ROUND CAROUSEL

	Price Paid	Value Of My Collection
1.		
2.		
3.		
4.		
5.		
6.		
7.		
PENCIL TOTALS		

⑦ New! #506206

Virginia
It's So Merry Going
'Round With You
Issued: 1999 • Current
Original Price: $20
Value by Year Mark:
8–$20 **9**–$20

Beta Is
For Bears

B

① #305995

Greek Alpha Bear
Issued: 1998 • Current
Original Price: $7.50
Value: $7.50

② #306002

Greek Beta Bear
Issued: 1998 • Current
Original Price: $7.50
Value: $7.50

③ #306010

Greek Gamma Bear
Issued: 1998 • Current
Original Price: $7.50
Value: $7.50

④ #306037

Greek Delta Bear
Issued: 1998 • Current
Original Price: $7.50
Value: $7.50

⑤ #306045

Greek Epsilon Bear
Issued: 1998 • Current
Original Price: $7.50
Value: $7.50

⑥ #306053

Greek Zeta Bear
Issued: 1998 • Current
Original Price: $7.50
Value: $7.50

⑦ #306088

Greek Eta Bear
Issued: 1998 • Current
Original Price: $7.50
Value: $7.50

⑧ #306096

Greek Theta Bear
Issued: 1998 • Current
Original Price: $7.50
Value: $7.50

BETA IS FOR BEARS

	Price Paid	Value Of My Collection
1.		
2.		
3.		
4.		
5.		
6.		
7.		
8.		
	PENCIL TOTALS	

BETA IS FOR BEARS

① #306118

Greek Iota Bear
Issued: 1998 • Current
Original Price: $7.50
Value: $7.50

② #306126

Greek Kappa Bear
Issued: 1998 • Current
Original Price: $7.50
Value: $7.50

③ #306134

Greek Lambda Bear
Issued: 1998 • Current
Original Price: $7.50
Value: $7.50

④ #306142

Greek Mu Bear
Issued: 1998 • Current
Original Price: $7.50
Value: $7.50

⑤ #306150

Greek Nu Bear
Issued: 1998 • Current
Original Price: $7.50
Value: $7.50

⑥ #306185

Greek Xi Bear
Issued: 1998 • Current
Original Price: $7.50
Value: $7.50

BETA IS FOR BEARS

	Price Paid	Value Of My Collection
1.		
2.		
3.		
4.		
5.		
6.		
7.		
8.		

PENCIL TOTALS

⑦ #306193

Greek Omicron Bear
Issued: 1998 • Current
Original Price: $7.50
Value: $7.50

⑧ #306207

Greek Pi Bear
Issued: 1998 • Current
Original Price: $7.50
Value: $7.50

BETA IS FOR BEARS

① #306215

Greek Rho Bear
Issued: 1998 • Current
Original Price: $7.50
Value: $7.50

② #306223

Greek Sigma Bear
Issued: 1998 • Current
Original Price: $7.50
Value: $7.50

③ #306231

Greek Tau Bear
Issued: 1998 • Current
Original Price: $7.50
Value: $7.50

④ #306258

Greek Upsilon Bear
Issued: 1998 • Current
Original Price: $7.50
Value: $7.50

⑤ #306266

Greek Phi Bear
Issued: 1998 • Current
Original Price: $7.50
Value: $7.50

⑥ #306274

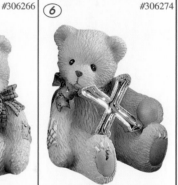

Greek Chi Bear
Issued: 1998 • Current
Original Price: $7.50
Value: $7.50

⑦ #306282

Greek Psi Bear
Issued: 1998 • Current
Original Price: $7.50
Value: $7.50

⑧ #306290

Greek Omega Bear
Issued: 1998 • Current
Original Price: $7.50
Value: $7.50

BETA IS FOR BEARS

	Price Paid	Value Of My Collection
1.		
2.		
3.		
4.		
5.		
6.		
7.		
8.		
PENCIL TOTALS		

Blossoms Of Friendship

① #202932

Dahlia
You're The Best Pick Of The Bunch
Issued: 1997 • Current
Original Price: $15
Value by Year Mark:
6–$25 **7**–$18 **8**–$15 **9**–$15

② #202908

Iris
You're The Iris Of My Eye
Issued: 1997 • Current
Original Price: $15
Value by Year Mark:
6–$25 **7**–$18 **8**–$15 **9**–$15

③ #202959

Lily
Lilies Bloom With Petals Of Hope
Issued: 1998 • Current
Original Price: $15
Value by Year Mark:
8–$15 **9**–$15

④ #202959A

Lily
(1997 Catalog Exclusive)
Lilies Bloom With Petals Of Hope
Issued: 1997 • Closed: 1997
Original Price: $15
Value by Year Mark: **7**–$45

⑤ #202967

Ornamental Furniture Figurines (set/3)
Issued: 1997 • Current
Original Price: $17.50
Value: $17.50

BLOSSOMS OF FRIENDSHIP

	Price Paid	Value Of My Collection
1.		
2.		
3.		
4.		
5.		
6.		
7.		

PENCIL TOTALS

⑥ #202886

Rose
Everything's Coming Up Roses
Issued: 1997 • Current
Original Price: $15
Value by Year Mark:
6–$25 **7**–$18 **8**–$15 **9**–$15

⑦ #202894

Susan
Love Stems From Our Friendship
Issued: 1997 • Current
Original Price: $15
Value by Year Mark:
6–$25 **7**–$18 **8**–$15 **9**–$15

By The Sea, By The Sea

① #203505

Gregg
*Everything Pails In
Comparison To Friends*
Issued: 1997 • Current
Original Price: $20
Value by Year Mark:
6–$28 **7**–$23 **8**–$20 **9**–$20

② #203475

Jerry
Ready To Make A Splash
Issued: 1997 • Current
Original Price: $17.50
Value by Year Mark:
6–$25 **7**–$20
8–$17.50 **9**–$17.50

③ #203513

Jim and Joey
*Underneath It All We're
Forever Friends*
Issued: 1997 • Current
Original Price: $25
Value by Year Mark:
6–$32 **7**–$28 **8**–$25 **9**–$25

④ #203491

Judy
I'm Your Bathing Beauty
Issued: 1997 • Current
Original Price: $35
Value by Year Mark:
6–$42 **7**–$38 **8**–$35 **9**–$35

⑤ #203467

Sandy
*There's Room In My
Sand Castle For You*
Issued: 1997 • Current
Original Price: $20
Value by Year Mark:
6–$26 **7**–$23 **8**–$20 **9**–$20

The Cherished Seasons

⑥ #203351

Gretchen
Winter Brings A Season Of Joy
Issued: 1997 • Current
Original Price: $25
Value by Year Mark:
7–$30 **8**–$25 **9**–$25

BY THE SEA, BY THE SEA

	Price Paid	Value Of My Collection
1.		
2.		
3.		
4.		
5.		

THE CHERISHED SEASONS

6.		

PENCIL TOTALS

① #203343

Hannah
Autumn Brings A Season Of Thanksgiving
Issued: 1997 • Current
Original Price: $20
Value by Year Mark:
7–$25 **8**–$20 **9**–$20

② #203335

Kimberly
Summer Brings A Season Of Warmth
Issued: 1997 • Current
Original Price: $22.50
Value by Year Mark:
7–$26 **8**–$22.50 **9**–$22.50

③ #203300

Megan
Spring Brings A Season Of Beauty
Issued: 1997 • Current
Original Price: $20
Value by Year Mark:
7–$25 **8**–$20 **9**–$20

Circus

④ #103713

Bruno
Step Right Up And Smile
Issued: 1996 • Current
Original Price: $17.50
Value by Year Mark:
5–$32 **6**–$25 **7**–$20
8–$17.50 **9**–$17.50

⑤ #103977

Circus Elephant With Bear
Trunk Full Of Bear Hugs
Issued: 1996 • Current
Original Price: $22.50
Value by Year Mark:
5–$33 **6**–$28 **7**–$25
8–$22.50 **9**–$22.50

THE CHERISHED SEASONS

	Price Paid	Value Of My Collection
1.		
2.		
3.		

CIRCUS

4.		
5.		
6.		

PENCIL TOTALS

⑥ #104256

Circus Tent With Rings

Wally   Claudia

Bruno

Circus Gift Set (set/5)
Issued: 1996 • Current
Original Price: $75
Value by Year Mark:
5–$118.50 **6**–$97.50 **7**–$82.50 **8**–$75 **9**–$75

1 #203548

Circus Lion
You're My Mane Attraction
Issued: 1997 • Current
Original Price: $12.50
Value by Year Mark:
6–$19 **7**–$14
8–$12.50 **9**–$12.50

2 #137596

Circus Seal With Ball
Seal Of Friendship
Issued: 1996 • Current
Original Price: $10
Value by Year Mark:
5–$23 **6**–$14 **7**–$12
8–$10 **9**–$10

3 #107700

Circus Tent With Rings (set/2)
Issued: 1996 • Current
Original Price: $22.50
Value: $22.50

4 #103721

Claudia
You Take The Center Ring With Me
Issued: 1996 • Current
Original Price: $17.50
Value by Year Mark:
5–$32 **6**–$25 **7**–$20
8–$17.50 **9**–$17.50

5 #111430

Clown On Ball (musical)
♪ *Put On A Happy Face*
Issued: 1996 • Current
Original Price: $40
Value: $40

6 #103748

Dudley
Just Clowning Around
Issued: 1997 • Current
Original Price: $17.50
Value by Year Mark:
6–$23 **7**–$20
8–$17.50 **9**–$17.50

7 #103756

Logan
Love Is A Bear Necessity
Issued: 1997 • Current
Original Price: $17.50
Value by Year Mark:
6–$24 **7**–$20
8–$17.50 **9**–$17.50
Variation: "Limited To Year Of Production" on understamp
Value: $45

CIRCUS

	Price Paid	Value Of My Collection
1.		
2.		
3.		
4.		
5.		
6.		
7.		
PENCIL TOTALS		

CIRCUS

(1) #203572

Shelby
Friendship Keeps You Popping
Issued: 1997 • Current
Original Price: $17.50
Value by Year Mark:
6–$23 **7**–$20
8–$17.50 **9**–$17.50

(2) #103942

Tonya (set/2)
Friends Are Bear Essentials
Issued: 1997 • Current
Original Price: $20
Value by Year Mark:
6–$28 **7**–$23 **8**–$20 **9**–$20

(3) #103934

Wally
You're The Tops With Me
Issued: 1996 • Current
Original Price: $17.50
Value by Year Mark:
5–$32 **6**–$25 **7**–$20
8–$17.50 **9**–$17.50

Count On Me

(4) #302945

Bear With 0 Block
Issued: 1998 • Current
Original Price: $5
Value: $5

(5) #302821

Bear With 1 Block
Issued: 1998 • Current
Original Price: $5
Value: $5

CIRCUS

	Price Paid	Value Of My Collection
1.		
2.		
3.		

COUNT ON ME

4.		
5.		
6.		
7.		

PENCIL TOTALS

(6) #302848

Bear With 2 Block
Issued: 1998 • Current
Original Price: $5
Value: $5

(7) #302856

Bear With 3 Block
Issued: 1998 • Current
Original Price: $5
Value: $5

COUNT/DICKENS

① #302864	② #302872	③ #302899

Bear With 4 Block Issued: 1998 • Current Original Price: $5 Value: $5	**Bear With 5 Block** Issued: 1998 • Current Original Price: $5 Value: $5	**Bear With 6 Block** Issued: 1998 • Current Original Price: $5 Value: $5

④ #302902	⑤ #302910	⑥ #302929

Bear With 7 Block Issued: 1998 • Current Original Price: $5 Value: $5	**Bear With 8 Block** Issued: 1998 • Current Original Price: $5 Value: $5	**Bear With 9 Block** Issued: 1998 • Current Original Price: $5 Value: $5

Dickens Village

⑦ #617326

Bear Cratchit
And A Very Merry Christmas
To You Mr. Scrooge
Issued: 1994 • Suspended: 1996
Original Price: $17.50
Value by Year Mark:
4–$42 **5**–$37 **6**–$27

COUNT ON ME

	Price Paid	Value Of My Collection
1.		
2.		
3.		
4.		
5.		
6.		

DICKENS VILLAGE

7.	17.50	42.00
	17.50	42.00
PENCIL TOTALS		

1 #614807

Gabriel

Garland

Gloria

Christmas Ghosts (set/3)
Issued: 1994 • Suspended: 1996
Original Price: $55
Value by Year Mark: **4**–$112 **5**–$95 **6**–$68

2 #651362

**The Cratchits House
(night light)**
Issued: 1994 • Suspended: 1996
Original Price: $75
Value: $100

3 #617296

Ebearnezer Scrooge
Bah Humbug!
Issued: 1994 • Suspended: 1996
Original Price: $17.50
Value by Year Mark:
4–$50 **5**–$36 **6**–$28

4 #614785

Jacob Bearly
*You Will Be Haunted By
Three Spirits*
Issued: 1994 • Suspended: 1996
Original Price: $17.50
Value by Year Mark:
4–$38 **5**–$32 **6**–$26

5 #617318

Mrs. Cratchit
*A Beary Christmas And A
Happy New Year!*
Issued: 1994 • Suspended: 1996
Original Price: $18.50
Value by Year Mark:
4–$45 **5**–$38 **6**–$28

DICKENS VILLAGE

	Price Paid	Value Of My Collection
1.		
2.		
3.	17.50	50.00
4.	17.50	38.00
5.	18.50	45.00
6.		
7.		
	53.50	133.00

PENCIL TOTALS

6 #622788

**Scrooge and Marley
Counting House
(night light)**
Issued: 1994 • Suspended: 1996
Original Price: $75
Value: $100

7 #614777

Tiny Ted-Bear
God Bless Us Everyone
Issued: 1994 • Suspended: 1996
Original Price: $10
Value by Year Mark:
4–$37 **5**–$30 **6**–$23

Down Strawberry Lane

① #202991

Diane (LE-1997)
I Picked The Beary Best For You
Issued: 1997 • Closed: 1997
Original Price: $25
Value by Year Mark: **7**–$42

② #156329

Ella
Love Grows In My Heart
Issued: 1996 • Current
Original Price: $15
Value by Year Mark:
5–$31 **6**–$23 **7**–$18
8–$15 **9**–$15

③ #156337

Jenna
You're Berry Special To Me
Issued: 1996 • Current
Original Price: $15
Value by Year Mark:
5–$32 **6**–$23 **7**–$18
8–$15 **9**–$15

④ #156299

Matthew
*A Dash Of Love Sweetens
Any Day!*
Issued: 1996 • Current
Original Price: $15
Value by Year Mark:
5–$32 **6**–$23 **7**–$18
8–$15 **9**–$15

⑤ #900931

**Strawberry Mini
Figurines (set/3)**
Issued: 1996 • Current
Original Price: $3.50
Value: $3.50

⑥ #156310

Tara
You're My Berry Best Friend!
Issued: 1996 • Current
Original Price: $15
Value by Year Mark:
5–$31 **6**–$23 **7**–$18
8–$15 **9**–$15

⑦ #156302

Thelma
Cozy Tea For Two
Issued: 1996 • Current
Original Price: $22.50
Value by Year Mark:
5–$43 **6**–$32 **7**–$25
8–$22.50 **9**–$22.50

DOWN STRAWBERRY LANE

	Price Paid	Value Of My Collection
1.	25.00	42.00
2.		
3.		
4.		
5.		
6.		
7.		
	25.00	42.00
PENCIL TOTALS		

Follow The Rainbow

① #302791

Carter and Elsie
We're Friends Rain Or Shine
Issued: 1998 • Current
Original Price: $35
Value by Year Mark:
7–$40 **8**–$35 **9**–$35

② #302775

Ellen
You Color My Rainbow
Issued: 1998 • Current
Original Price: $20
Value by Year Mark:
7–$23 **8**–$20 **9**–$20

③ #310409

Follow The Rainbow Mini Accessories (set/4)
Issued: 1998 • Current
Original Price: $10
Value: $10

④ #302767

Joyce
Plant A Rainbow And Watch It Grow
Issued: 1998 • Current
Original Price: $25
Value by Year Mark:
7–$28 **8**–$25 **9**–$25

Friends Come In All Shades And Sizes

FOLLOW THE RAINBOW

	Price Paid	Value Of My Collection
1.		
2.		
3.		
4.		

FRIENDS COME IN ALL SHADES AND SIZES

5.		
6.		

PENCIL TOTALS

⑤ #476714

PHOTO UNAVAILABLE

Cole (1998 Event Exclusive)
We've Got A Lot To Be Thankful For
Issued: 1998 • Closed: 1998
Original Price: $12.50
Value by Year Mark: **8**–N/E

⑥ #476714R

Cole (1998 Event Exclusive, Rare Bear)
We've Got A Lot To Be Thankful For
Issued: 1998 • Closed: 1998
Original Price: $12.50
Value by Year Mark: **8**–N/E

① #476722

PHOTO UNAVAILABLE

Marty (1998 Event Exclusive)
I'll Always Be There For You
Issued: 1998 • Closed: 1998
Original Price: $12.50
Value by Year Mark: **8**–N/E

② #476722R

Marty (1998 Event Exclusive, Rare Bear)
I'll Always Be There For You
Issued: 1998 • Closed: 1998
Original Price: $12.50
Value by Year Mark: **8**–N/E

③ #476706

PHOTO UNAVAILABLE

Miranda (1998 Event Exclusive)
No Matter How Blue You Feel, A Hug Can Heal
Issued: 1998 • Closed: 1998
Original Price: $12.50
Value by Year Mark: **8**–N/E

④ #476706R

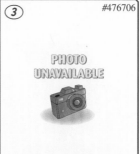

Miranda (1998 Event Exclusive, Rare Bear)
No Matter How Blue You Feel, A Hug Can Heal
Issued: 1998 • Closed: 1998
Original Price: $12.50
Value by Year Mark: **8**–N/E

⑤ #476595

PHOTO UNAVAILABLE

Tanna (1998 Event Exclusive)
When Your Hands Are Full, There's Still Room In Your Heart
Issued: 1998 • Closed: 1998
Original Price: $12.50
Value by Year Mark: **8**–N/E

⑥ #476595R

Tanna (1998 Event Exclusive, Rare Bear)
When Your Hands Are Full, There's Still Room In Your Heart
Issued: 1998 • Closed: 1998
Original Price: $12.50
Value by Year Mark: **8**–N/E

Happily Ever After

⑦ #302465

Alicia
Through The Looking Glass, I See You!
Issued: 1998 • Current
Original Price: $22.50
Value by Year Mark:
7–$24 **8**–$22.50 **9**–$22.50

FRIENDS COME IN ALL SHADES AND SIZES

	Price Paid	Value Of My Collection
1.		
2.		
3.		
4.		
5.		
6.		

HAPPILY EVER AFTER

7.		
PENCIL TOTALS		

① #302457

Brett
Come To Neverland With Me
Issued: 1998 • Current
Original Price: $22.50
Value by Year Mark:
7–$24 **8**–$22.50 **9**–$22.50

② #302473

Christina
I Found My Prince In You
Issued: 1998 • Current
Original Price: $22.50
Value by Year Mark:
7–$24 **8**–$22.50 **9**–$22.50

③ #302481

Harvey and Gigi
Finding The Path To Your Heart
Issued: 1998 • Current
Original Price: $30
Value by Year Mark:
7–$33 **8**–$30 **9**–$30

④ #302570

Kelsie
Be The Apple Of My Eye
Issued: 1998 • Current
Original Price: $20
Value by Year Mark:
7–$22 **8**–$20 **9**–$20

⑤ #302511

Lois
To Grandmother's House We Go
Issued: 1998 • Current
Original Price: $22.50
Value by Year Mark:
7–$24 **8**–$22.50 **9**–$22.50

⑥ #476463

New!

Pinocchio
*You've Got My Heart
On A String*
Issued: 1999 • Current
Original Price: $30
Value by Year Mark:
8–$30 **9**–$30

HAPPILY EVER AFTER

	Price Paid	Value Of My Collection
1.		
2.		
3.		
4.		
5.		
6.		
7.		
PENCIL TOTALS		

⑦ #481696

New!

Winnie
You're My Perfect Prince
Issued: 1999 • Current
Original Price: $17.50
Value by Year Mark:
8–$17.50 **9**–$17.50

Holiday Dangling

#176168

Ho Ho Blocks (ornament)
Issued: 1996 • Suspended: 1997
Original Price: $12.50
Value: $18

#176095

Holden
Catchin' The Holiday Spirit!
Issued: 1996 • Suspended: 1997
Original Price: $15
Value by Year Mark:
6–$23 **7**–$19

#176133

Jolene
Dropping You A Holiday Greeting
Issued: 1996 • Suspended: 1997
Original Price: $20
Value by Year Mark:
6–$28 **7**–$23

#176087

Joy
You Always Bring Joy
Issued: 1996 • Suspended: 1997
Original Price: $15
Value by Year Mark:
6–$23 **7**–$19

#176168

Joy Blocks (ornament)
Issued: 1996 • Suspended: 1997
Original Price: $12.50
Value: $16

#176109

Noel
An Old-Fashioned Noel To You
Issued: 1996 • Suspended: 1997
Original Price: $15
Value by Year Mark:
6–$26 **7**–$20

#176141

Nolan
A String Of Good Tidings
Issued: 1996 • Suspended: 1997
Original Price: $20
Value by Year Mark:
6–$27 **7**–$23

HOLIDAY DANGLING

	Price Paid	Value Of My Collection
1.		
2.		
3.		
4.	15.00	23.00
5.		
6.		
7.		
	15.00	23.00
PENCIL TOTALS		

Just Between Friends

#303127 ①

Bear With Banner
I Miss You
Issued: 1998 • Current
Original Price: $7.50
Value: $7.50

#303100 ②

**Bear With Books
And Crayon**
Forgive Me
Issued: 1998 • Current
Original Price: $7.50
Value: $7.50

#303135 ③

**Bear With Paint
And Brush**
Please Smile
Issued: 1998 • Current
Original Price: $7.50
Value: $7.50

#303097 ④

Bear With Pillow
I'm Sorry
Issued: 1998 • Current
Original Price: $7.50
Value: $7.50

#303143 ⑤

Bear With Scroll
Good Luck
Issued: 1998 • Current
Original Price: $7.50
Value: $7.50

JUST BETWEEN FRIENDS

	Price Paid	Value Of My Collection
1.		
2.		
3.		
4.		
5.		
6.		
7.		

PENCIL TOTALS

#303119 ⑥

Bear With Sign
What A Day! Everything's Ok
Issued: 1998 • Current
Original Price: $7.50
Value: $7.50

#303151 ⑦

Mini Risers (set/3)
Issued: 1998 • Current
Original Price: $12
Value: $12

Let Heaven And Nature Sing

① *Future Release!* #533904

Emma (LE-2000)
Let Earth Proclaim Its Peace
To Be Issued: 2000
Original Price: $20
Value by Year Mark: N/E

② *New!* #533890

Felicia (LE-1999)
Joy To The World
Issued: 1999
To Be Closed: 1999
Original Price: $20
Value by Year Mark: **9**–$20

③ *Future Release!* #533912

Rebecca (LE-2001)
Let Heaven And Nature Sing
To Be Issued: 2001
Original Price: $20
Value by Year Mark: N/E

Little Sparkles

④ #239720

Bear With January Birthstone
Issued: 1997 • Current
Original Price: $7.50
Value: $7.50

⑤ #239747

Bear With February Birthstone
Issued: 1997 • Current
Original Price: $7.50
Value: $7.50

⑥ #239763

Bear With March Birthstone
Issued: 1997 • Current
Original Price: $7.50
Value: $7.50

LET HEAVEN AND NATURE SING		
	Price Paid	Value Of My Collection
1.		
2.		
3.		
LITTLE SPARKLES		
4.		
5.		
6.		
PENCIL TOTALS		

LET HEAVEN/LITTLE

① #239771

Bear With April Birthstone
Issued: 1997 • Current
Original Price: $7.50
Value: $7.50

② #239798

Bear With May Birthstone
Issued: 1997 • Current
Original Price: $7.50
Value: $7.50

③ #239801

Bear With June Birthstone
Issued: 1997 • Current
Original Price: $7.50
Value: $7.50

④ #239828

Bear With July Birthstone
Issued: 1997 • Current
Original Price: $7.50
Value: $7.50

⑤ #239836

Bear With August Birthstone
Issued: 1997 • Current
Original Price: $7.50
Value: $7.50

⑥ #239844

Bear With September Birthstone
Issued: 1997 • Current
Original Price: $7.50
Value: $7.50

LITTLE SPARKLES

	Price Paid	Value Of My Collection
1.		
2.		
3.		
4.		
5.		
6.		
7.		
8.		

PENCIL TOTALS

⑦ #239852

Bear With October Birthstone
Issued: 1997 • Current
Original Price: $7.50
Value: $7.50

⑧ #239860

Bear With November Birthstone
Issued: 1997 • Current
Original Price: $7.50
Value: $7.50

① #239933

**Bear With December
Birthstone**
Issued: 1997 • Current
Original Price: $7.50
Value: $7.50

*Love Letters
From Teddie*

② #203084

Heart Dangling Blocks
Issued: 1997 • Current
Original Price: $7.50
Value: $7.50

③ #902950

I Love Bears Letters
Issued: 1997 • Current
Original Price: $7.50
Value: $7.50

④ #902969

I Love Hugs Letters
Issued: 1997 • Current
Original Price: $7.50
Value: $7.50

⑤ #156515

I Love You Letters
Issued: 1997 • Current
Original Price: $7.50
Value: $7.50

⑥ #203076

Love Blocks
Issued: 1997 • Current
Original Price: $13.50
Value: $13.50

⑦ #240281

**Love Letters Display
Blocks (set/3)**
Issued: 1997 • Current
Original Price: $20
Value: $20

LITTLE SPARKLES

	Price Paid	Value Of My Collection
1.		

LOVE LETTERS FROM TEDDIE

2.		
3.		
4.		
5.		
6.		
7.		

PENCIL TOTALS

LITTLE/LOVE

M®nthly Friends To Cherish

① #914789

Alan (April)
Showers Of Friendship
Issued: 1995 • Current
Original Price: $15
Value by Year Mark:
4–$44 **5**–$35 **6**–$22
7–$18 **8**–$15 **9**–$15

② #914827

Arthur (August)
Smooth Sailing
Issued: 1995 • Current
Original Price: $15
Value by Year Mark:
4–$38 **5**–$30 **6**–$24
7–$18 **8**–$15 **9**–$15

---

③ #914878

Denise (December)
Happy Holidays, Friend
Issued: 1995 • Current
Original Price: $15
Value by Year Mark:
4–$42 **5**–$33 **6**–$22
7–$18 **8**–$15 **9**–$15

---

④ #914754

Jack (January)
A New Year With Old Friends
Issued: 1995 • Current
Original Price: $15
Value by Year Mark:
4–$42 **5**–$32 **6**–$22
7–$18 **8**–$15 **9**–$15

---

⑤ #914819

Julie (July)
A Day In The Park
Issued: 1995 • Current
Original Price: $15
Value by Year Mark:
4–$38 **5**–$31 **6**–$22
7–$18 **8**–$15 **9**–$15

MONTHLY FRIENDS TO CHERISH

	Price Paid	Value Of My Collection
1.		
2.		
3.		
4.		
5.		
6.		
7.		
PENCIL TOTALS		

---

⑥ #914800

June (June)
Planting The Seed Of Friendship
Issued: 1995 • Current
Original Price: $15
Value by Year Mark:
4–$40 **5**–$30 **6**–$22
7–$18 **8**–$15 **9**–$15

---

⑦ #914770

Mark (March)
Friendship Is In The Air
Issued: 1995 • Current
Original Price: $15
Value by Year Mark:
4–$38 **5**–$30 **6**–$22
7–$18 **8**–$15 **9**–$15
Variation: tail on kite
Value by Year Mark: **5**–$45

MONTHLY/NATIVITY

① #914797

May (May)
Friendship Is In Bloom
Issued: 1995 • Current
Original Price: $15
Value by Year Mark:
4–$40 **5**–$30 **6**–$22
7–$18 **8**–$15 **9**–$15

② #914851

Nicole (November)
Thanks For Friends
Issued: 1995 • Current
Original Price: $15
Value by Year Mark:
4–$43 **5**–$33 **6**–$22
7–$18 **8**–$15 **9**–$15

③ #914843

Oscar (October)
Sweet Treats
Issued: 1995 • Current
Original Price: $15
Value by Year Mark:
4–$42 **5**–$33 **6**–$22
7–$18 **8**–$15 **9**–$15

④ #914762

Phoebe (February)
Be Mine
Issued: 1995 • Current
Original Price: $15
Value by Year Mark:
4–$43 **5**–$34 **6**–$23
7–$18 **8**–$15 **9**–$15

⑤ #914835

Seth (September)
School Days
Issued: 1995 • Current
Original Price: $15
Value by Year Mark:
4–$40 **5**–$30 **6**–$22
7–$18 **8**–$15 **9**–$15

Nativity

⑥ #912980

**Angel With Bells
(ornament)**
Issued: 1993 • Suspended: 1996
Original Price: $12.50
Value: $19

⑦ #912980

**Angel With Harp
(ornament)**
Issued: 1993 • Suspended: 1996
Original Price: $12.50
Value: $21

	MONTHLY FRIENDS TO CHERISH	
	Price Paid	Value Of My Collection
1.		
2.		
3.		
4.		
5.		
	NATIVITY	
6.		
7.		
	PENCIL TOTALS	

① #912980

**Angel With Trumpet
(ornament)**
Issued: 1993 • Suspended: 1996
Original Price: $12.50
Value: $21

② #951137

Angie
I Brought The Star
Issued: 1992 • Current
Original Price: $15
Value by Year Mark:
3–$66 **4**–$43 **5**–$35 **6**–$20
7–$17 **8**–$15 **9**–$15
Variation: gold metal halo
Value: **LETTER**–$95

③ #141267

Celeste
An Angel To Watch Over You
Issued: 1995 • Current
Original Price: $20
Value by Year Mark:
5–$40 **6**–$31 **7**–$22
8–$20 **9**–$20

④ #951218

**Creche With Coverlet
(set/2)**
Issued: 1992 • Current
Original Price: $50
Value: $50

⑤ #950688

**Maria With Baby/Josh
(set/2)**
Issued: 1992 • Current
Original Price: $35
Value by Year Mark:
LETTER–$100 **3**–$74 **4**–$50
5–$46 **6**–$42 **7**–$38
8–$35 **9**–$35

⑥ #914746

Mini Nativity With Creche
Our Love Is In The Highlands
Issued: 1993
Out Of Production: 1995
Original Price: $32.50
Value: $90

NATIVITY

	Price Paid	Value Of My Collection
1.		
2.		
3.		
4.		
5.		
6.		
7.		
PENCIL TOTALS		

⑦ #903485

**Nativity
(revolving musical)**
♪ *Silent Night*
Issued: 1993
Out Of Production: 1994
Original Price: $85
Value: $170

1 #916684

Angie

Creche With
Coverlet

Maria With
Baby/Josh

Nativity Collector Set (set/5)
Issued: 1993 • Current
Original Price: $100
Value by Year Mark:
LETTER–$245 **3**–$190 **4**–$143 **5**–$131 **6**–$112
7–$105 **8**–$100 **9**–$100

2 #176362

"The
Cherished One"

Nativity Prayer (plaque)
Issued: 1996 • Current
Original Price: $13.50
Value: $13.50

3 #904309

Nativity Pull Toy, Camel
*Friends Like You Are
Precious And True*
Issued: 1993 • Retired: 1997
Original Price: $30
Value: $52

4 #651095

Nativity Pull Toy, Cow
That's What Friends Are For
Issued: 1994 • Retired: 1997
Original Price: $22.50
Value by Year Mark:
4–$52 **5**–$44 **6**–$38

5 #912867

Nativity Pull Toys (set/2)
Issued: 1993 • Current
Original Price: $13.50
Value: $13.50

6 #912905

Ronnie
I'll Play My Drum For You
Issued: 1994 • Current
Original Price: $13.50
Value by Year Mark:
4–$38 **5**–$30 **6**–$18
7–$15 **8**–$13.50 **9**–$13.50

7 #950726

Sammy
Little Lambs Are In My Care
Issued: 1992 • Current
Original Price: $17.50
Value by Year Mark:
LETTER–$58 **3**–$48 **4**–$40
5–$34 **6**–$22 **7**–$20
8–$17.50 **9**–$17.50

NATIVITY

	Price Paid	Value Of My Collection
1.		
2.		
3.		
4.		
5.		
6.		
7.		
PENCIL TOTALS		

①

Edward
With Donkey

Richard
With Camel

Wilbur
With Teddy

#950718

Three Kings (set/3)
Issued: 1992 • Current
Original Price: $55
Value by Year Mark:
LETTER–$160 **3**–$95 **4**–$82 **5**–$62
6–$60 **7**–$57 **8**–$55 **9**–$55

Nursery Rhyme Series

② #624772

Jack & Jill
Our Friendship Will Never Tumble
Issued: 1994 • Retired: 1998
Original Price: $30
Value by Year Mark:
3–$64 **4**–$50 **5**–$43
6–$35 **7**–$33 **8**–$32

③ #624802

Little Bo Peep
Looking For A Friend Like You
Issued: 1994 • Retired: 1998
Original Price: $22.50
Value by Year Mark:
3–$56 **4**–$49 **5**–$40
6–$32 **7**–$25 **8**–$24

④ #624780

Little Jack Horner
*I'm Plum Happy You're
My Friend*
Issued: 1994 • Retired: 1998
Original Price: $20
Value by Year Mark:
3–$52 **4**–$45 **5**–$38
6–$30 **7**–$25 **8**–$24

NATIVITY

	Price Paid	Value Of My Collection
1.		

NURSERY RHYME SERIES

2.		
3.		
4.		
5.		
6.		

PENCIL TOTALS

⑤ #624799

Little Miss Muffet
*I'm Never Afraid With You
At My Side*
Issued: 1994 • Retired: 1998
Original Price: $20
Value by Year Mark:
3–$54 **4**–$47 **5**–$38
6–$27 **7**–$23 **8**–$22

⑥ #626074

Mary, Mary, Quite Contrary
*Friendship Blooms With
Loving Care*
Issued: 1994 • Retired: 1998
Original Price: $22.50
Value by Year Mark:
3–$60 **4**–$53 **5**–$44
6–$32 **7**–$25 **8**–$24

① #624810

Tom, Tom The Piper's Son
Wherever You Go, I'll Follow
Issued: 1994 • Retired: 1998
Original Price: $20
Value by Year Mark:
3–$54 **4**–$47 **5**–$38
6–$27 **7**–$23 **8**–$22

Nutcracker Suite

② #272132

Functional Nutcracker
Issued: 1997 • Current
Original Price: $90
Value: $90

③ #272388

Clara
Boy Prince
Herr Drosselmeyer
Mouse King

Nutcracker Suite Collector Set (set/4, LE-1997)
Issued: 1997 • Closed: 1997
Original Price: $70
Value by Year Mark: **7**–$86

④ #279641

Nutcracker Suite Furniture Figurines (set/2)
Issued: 1997 • Current
Original Price: $40
Value: $40

⑤ #292494

Nutcracker Suite Tree Musical
♪ *Dance Of The Sugar-Plum Fairy*
Issued: 1997 • Current
Original Price: $45
Value: $45

NURSERY RHYME SERIES		
	Price Paid	Value Of My Collection
1.		
NUTCRACKER SUITE		
2.		
3.		
4.		
5.		
PENCIL TOTALS		

NURSERY/NUTCRACKER

Old Fashioned Country Christmas

① New! #533769

Annette
Tender Care Given Here
Issued: 1999 • Current
Original Price: $20
Value by Year Mark:
8–$20 **9**–$20

② New! #533807

Brian
Look Out Snow! Here We Go!
Issued: 1999 • Current
Original Price: $22.50
Value by Year Mark:
8–$22.50 **9**–$22.50

③ New! #533823

Country Christmas Accessories (set/3)
Issued: 1999 • Current
Original Price: $30
Value: $30

④ New! #533793

Justin
We Share Forever, Whatever The Weather
Issued: 1999 • Current
Original Price: $20
Value by Year Mark:
8–$20 **9**–$20

⑤ New! #533777

Shirley
These Are The Best Kind Of Days
Issued: 1999 • Current
Original Price: $20
Value by Year Mark:
8–$20 **9**–$20

OLD FASHIONED COUNTRY CHRISTMAS

	Price Paid	Value Of My Collection
1.		
2.		
3.		
4.		
5.		
6.		

PENCIL TOTALS

⑥ New! #533785

Suzanne
Home Sweet Country Home
Issued: 1999 • Current
Original Price: $20
Value by Year Mark:
8–$20 **9**–$20

Our Cherished Day

① New! #476315

**A Beary Special
Groom-To-Be**
Issued: 1999 • Current
Original Price: $15
Value by Year Mark:
8–$15 **9**–$15

② New! #476285

**Beautiful And Bearly
Blushing**
Issued: 1999 • Current
Original Price: $15
Value by Year Mark:
8–$15 **9**–$15

③ New! #476382

**I've Got The Most
Important Job!**
Issued: 1999 • Current
Original Price: $9
Value by Year Mark:
8–$9 **9**–$9

④ New! #510254

*A Beary
Special
Groom-To-Be*

*Beautiful
And Bearly
Blushing*

Our Cherished Wedding Collectors Set (set/3)
Issued: 1999 • Current
Original Price: $50
Value by Year Mark: **8**–$50 **9**–$50

⑤ New! #476323

**So Glad To Be Part Of
Your Special Day**
Issued: 1999 • Current
Original Price: $10
Value by Year Mark:
8–$10 **9**–$10

⑥ New! #476374

**Sweet Flowers For
The Bride**
Issued: 1999 • Current
Original Price: $9
Value by Year Mark:
8–$9 **9**–$9

⑦ New! #476366

**The Time Has Come For
Wedding Bliss**
Issued: 1999 • Current
Original Price: $10
Value by Year Mark:
8–$10 **9**–$10

OUR CHERISHED DAY

	Price Paid	Value Of My Collection
1.	15.00	15.00
2.	15.00	15.00
3.		
4.		
5.	10.00	10.00
6.		
7.	10.00	10.00
	50.00	50.00

PENCIL TOTALS

Our Cherished Family

① #127922

Baby Boy
A Gift To Behold
Issued: 1998 • Current
Original Price: $7.50
Value by Year Mark:
7–$9 **8**–$7.50 **9**–$7.50

② #599352

Baby Girl
A Gift To Behold
Issued: 1998 • Current
Original Price: $7.50
Value by Year Mark:
7–$9 **8**–$7.50 **9**–$7.50

③ #624888

Father
A Father Is The Bearer Of Strength
Issued: 1994 • Current
Original Price: $13.50
Value by Year Mark:
3–$29 **4**–$25 **5**–$22 **6**–$18
7–$15 **8**–$13.50 **9**–$13.50

④ #127914

Grandma
Grandma Is God's Special Gift
Issued: 1998 • Current
Original Price: $17.50
Value by Year Mark:
7–$19 **8**–$17.50 **9**–$17.50

⑤ #127906

Grandpa
Grandpa Is God's Special Gift
Issued: 1998 • Current
Original Price: $17.50
Value by Year Mark:
7–$19 **8**–$17.50 **9**–$17.50

OUR CHERISHED FAMILY

	Price Paid	Value Of My Collection
1.		
2.		
3.		
4.		
5.		
6.		
7.		
PENCIL TOTALS		

⑥ #624861

Mother
A Mother's Love Bears All Things
Issued: 1994 • Current
Original Price: $20
Value by Year Mark:
3–$37 **4**–$32 **5**–$28 **6**–$25
7–$22 **8**–$20 **9**–$20
Variation: "Mum" on bottom
Value by Year Mark: **4**–$55

⑦ #624845

Older Daughter
Child Of Love
Issued: 1994 • Current
Original Price: $10
Value by Year Mark:
3–$28 **4**–$24 **5**–$20 **6**–$15
7–$12 **8**–$10 **9**–$10

① #624829

Older Son
Child Of Pride
Issued: 1994 • Current
Original Price: $10
Value by Year Mark:
3–$26 **4**–$22 **5**–$17 **6**–$14
7–$12 **8**–$10 **9**–$10

② #651125

Display

Father   Mother   Young   Young
                         Daughter   Son

Older Daughter   Older Son

Our Cherished Family Collector Set (set/7)
Issued: 1994 • Current
Original Price: $85
Value by Year Mark:
3–$176 **4**–$143 **5**–$121 **6**–$98 **7**–$85 **8**–$85 **9**–$85

③ #624853

Young Daughter
Child Of Kindness
Issued: 1994 • Current
Original Price: $9
Value by Year Mark:
3–$28 **4**–$20 **5**–$17 **6**–$13
7–$10 **8**–$9 **9**–$9

④ #624837

Young Son
Child Of Hope
Issued: 1994 • Current
Original Price: $9
Value by Year Mark:
3–$28 **4**–$20 **5**–$17 **6**–$13
7–$10 **8**–$9 **9**–$9

Our Cherished Neighbearhood

⑤ #352667

Christmas Decorated House
Issued: 1998 • Current
Original Price: $20
Value by Year Mark:
8–$20 **9**–$20

⑥ #352691

Neighbearhood Accessories (set/3)
Issued: 1998 • Current
Original Price: $15
Value: $15

OUR CHERISHED FAMILY

	Price Paid	Value Of My Collection
1.		
2.		
3.		
4.	9.00	28.00

OUR CHERISHED NEIGHBEARHOOD

5.		
6.		
	9.00	28.00
PENCIL TOTALS		

OUR/OUR

① #352659

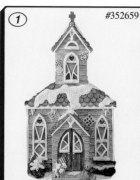

Winter Church Building
Issued: 1998 • Current
Original Price: $20
Value by Year Mark:
8–$20 **9**–$20

② #352675

Winter Post Office Building
Issued: 1998 • Current
Original Price: $20
Value by Year Mark:
8–$20 **9**–$20

③ #352683

Winter Train Depot Building
Issued: 1998 • Current
Original Price: $20
Value by Year Mark:
8–$20 **9**–$20

Santa Express

④ #219525

Casey
Friendship Is The Perfect End To The Holidays
Issued: 1996 • Retired: 1998
Original Price: $22.50
Value by Year Mark:
6–$34 **7**–$26 **8**–$24

⑤ #219177

Cindy
This Train Is Bound For Holiday Surprises!
Issued: 1997 • Retired: 1998
Original Price: $17.50
Value by Year Mark:
7–$28 **8**–$20

OUR CHERISHED NEIGHBEARHOOD

	Price Paid	Value Of My Collection
1.		
2.		
3.		

SANTA EXPRESS

4.		
5.		
6.		
7.		

PENCIL TOTALS

⑥ #219088

Colin
He Knows If You've Been Bad Or Good
Issued: 1996 • Retired: 1998
Original Price: $17.50
Value by Year Mark:
6–$32 **7**–$24 **8**–$20

⑦ #219118

Kirby
Heading Into The Holidays With Deer Friends
Issued: 1997 • Retired: 1998
Original Price: $17.50
Value by Year Mark:
7–$28 **8**–$20

① #269891

**Lamppost Lights
(accessory)**
Issued: 1997
Out Of Production: 1998
Original Price: $10
Value: N/E

② #219061

Lionel
All Aboard The Santa Express
Issued: 1996 • Retired: 1998
Original Price: $22.50
Value by Year Mark:
6–$34 **7**–$26 **8**–$24

③ #219312

Nick
*Ho, Ho, Ho – To The
Holidays We Go!*
Issued: 1997 • Retired: 1998
Original Price: $17.50
Value by Year Mark:
7–$28 **8**–$20

④ #935557

**Santa Express Accessory
Set (set/11)**
Issued: 1996
Out Of Production: 1998
Original Price: $30
Value: N/E

⑤ #269905

Snow Bear
Issued: 1997
Out Of Production: 1998
Original Price: $12.50
Value by Year Mark:
7–$20 **8**–$16

⑥ #269913

Street Lamp And Bear
Issued: 1997
Out Of Production: 1998
Original Price: $15
Value by Year Mark:
7–$23 **8**–$19

⑦ #219487

Tony
A First Class Delivery For You
Issued: 1996 • Retired: 1998
Original Price: $17.50
Value by Year Mark:
6–$34 **7**–$25 **8**–$20

⑧ #219096

Toy Car
*Rolling Along With
Friends And Smiles*
Issued: 1996 • Retired: 1998
Original Price: $17.50
Value by Year Mark:
6–$26 **7**–$22 **8**–$20

	Price Paid	Value Of My Collection
SANTA EXPRESS		
1.		
2.		
3.		
4.		
5.		
6.		
7.		
8.		
PENCIL TOTALS		

Santa Series

① #176036

Klaus (LE-1996)
Bearer Of Good Tidings
Issued: 1996 • Closed: 1996
Original Price: $20
Value by Year Mark: **6**–$48

② #272140

Kris (LE-1997)
Up On The Rooftop
Issued: 1997 • Closed: 1997
Original Price: $22.50
Value by Year Mark: **7**–$39

③ #141100

Nickolas (LE-1995)
You're At The Top Of My List
Issued: 1995 • Closed: 1995
Original Price: $20
Value by Year Mark: **5**–$64

④ #534242

New!

Sanford (LE-1999)
Celebrate Family, Friends And Tradition
Issued: 1999
To Be Closed: 1999
Original Price: $25
Value by Year Mark: **9**–$25

⑤ #352713

Santa (LE-1998)
A Little Holiday R & R
Issued: 1998 • Closed: 1998
Original Price: $22.50
Value by Year Mark: **8**–$34

SANTA SERIES

	Price Paid	Value Of My Collection
1.	20.00	48.00
2.	22.50	39.00
3.	20.00	64.00
4.		
5.		

SANTA'S WORKSHOP

6.		
	62.50	151.00

PENCIL TOTALS

Santa's Workshop

⑥ #176079

Christmas Mini Figurines (set/3)
Issued: 1996 • Current
Original Price: $15
Value: $15

Elf Riding Candy Cane (ornament)
#651389
Issued: 1995 • Suspended: 1996
Original Price: $12.50
Value: $27

Elf With Doll (ornament)
#625434
Issued: 1995 • Suspended: 1996
Original Price: $12.50
Value: $27

Elf With Stuffed Reindeer (ornament)
#625442
Issued: 1995 • Suspended: 1996
Original Price: $12.50
Value: $27

Ginger
#141127
Painting Your Holidays With Love
Issued: 1995 • Retired: 1998
Original Price: $22.50
Value by Year Mark:
5–$47 **6**–$33 **7**–$27 **8**–$25

Holly
#141119
A Cup Of Homemade Love
Issued: 1995 • Retired: 1998
Original Price: $18.50
Value by Year Mark:
5–$42 **6**–$28 **7**–$24 **8**–$21

Meri
#141135
Handsewn Holidays
Issued: 1995 • Retired: 1998
Original Price: $20
Value by Year Mark:
5–$52 **6**–$34 **7**–$25 **8**–$23

Mrs. Claus Bear (ornament)
#625426
Issued: 1995 • Suspended: 1996
Original Price: $12.50
Value: $27

SANTA'S WORKSHOP

	Price Paid	Value Of My Collection
1.		
2.		
3.		
4.	22.50	47.00
5.	2	
6.	20.00	52.00
7.		
	42.50	99.00

PENCIL TOTALS

SANTA'S WORKSHOP

1 #651370

Santa Bear (ornament)
Issued: 1995 • Current
Original Price: $12.50
Value: $12.50

2 #141925

Santa's Workshop (night light)
Issued: 1995 • Current
Original Price: $75
Value: $75

3 #141143

Yule
Building A Sturdy Friendship
Issued: 1995 • Retired: 1998
Original Price: $22.50
Value by Year Mark:
5–$52 **6**–$37 **7**–$27 **8**–$25

School Days

4 #477036
New!

School Days Mini Figurines (4 asst.)
Boy In Baseball Hat
Issued: 1999 • Current
Original Price: $7.50
Value: $7.50

5 #477036
New!

School Days Mini Figurines (4 asst.)
Boy With Book And Apple
Issued: 1999 • Current
Original Price: $7.50
Value: $7.50

Santa's Workshop

	Price Paid	Value Of My Collection
1.		
2.		
3.		

School Days

4.		
5.		
6.		
7.		

PENCIL TOTALS

6 #477036
New!

School Days Mini Figurines (4 asst.)
Girl With Apple And Flag
Issued: 1999 • Current
Original Price: $7.50
Value: $7.50

7 #477036
New!

School Days Mini Figurines (4 asst.)
Girl With Pom Poms
Issued: 1999 • Current
Original Price: $7.50
Value: $7.50

① New! #477044

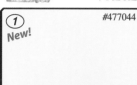

School Days Plaque
Issued: 1999 • Current
Original Price: $8
Value: $8

Sugar & Spice

**② ** #352586

Missy, Cookie & Riley
*A Special Recipe For
Our Friendship*
Issued: 1998 • Current
Original Price: $35
Value by Year Mark:
8–$35 **9**–$35

**③ ** #352616

Pamela and Grayson
*A Dash Of Love To
Warm Your Heart*
Issued: 1998 • Current
Original Price: $22.50
Value by Year Mark:
8–$22.50 **9**–$22.50

**④ ** #352594

Sharon
Sweetness Pours From My Heart
Issued: 1998 • Current
Original Price: $20
Value by Year Mark:
8–$20 **9**–$20

**⑤ ** #362417

**Sugar & Spice Mini
Accessories (set/6)**
Issued: 1998 • Current
Original Price: $15
Value: $15

**⑥ ** #352608

Wayne
Spoonfuls Of Sweetness
Issued: 1998 • Current
Original Price: $20
Value by Year Mark:
8–$20 **9**–$20

*Sweetheart
Ball*

SCHOOL DAYS

	Price Paid	Value Of My Collection
1.		

SUGAR & SPICE

2.		
3.		
4.		
5.		
6.		

PENCIL TOTALS

1 #156485

Craig and Cheri
Sweethearts Forever
Issued: 1996 • Current
Original Price: $25
Value by Year Mark:
5–$50 **6**–$35 **7**–$28
8–$25 **9**–$25

2 #156469

Darla
My Heart Wishes For You
Issued: 1996 • Current
Original Price: $20
Value by Year Mark:
5–$45 **6**–$30 **7**–$25
8–$20 **9**–$20

3 #156450

Darrel
Love Unveils A Happy Heart
Issued: 1996 • Current
Original Price: $17.50
Value by Year Mark:
5–$42 **6**–$28 **7**–$22
8–$17.50 **9**–$17.50

4 #156477

Jilly
Won't You Be My Sweetheart?
Issued: 1996 • Current
Original Price: $17.50
Value by Year Mark:
5–$45 **6**–$26 **7**–$22
8–$17.50 **9**–$17.50

5 #302732

Trellis Display

Harry

Katherine

King And Queen Of Hearts Collector Set
(set/3, LE-9/97-8/98)
Issued: 1997 • Closed: 1998
Original Price: $65
Value by Year Mark: **7**–$77 **8**–$70

SWEETHEART BALL

	Price Paid	Value Of My Collection
1.	25.00	25.00
2.		
3.		
4.	17.50	45.00
5.		
6.		
7.		
	42.50	70.00

PENCIL TOTALS

6 #156442

Marian
You're The Hero Of My Heart
Issued: 1996 • Current
Original Price: $20
Value by Year Mark:
5–$52 **6**–$32 **7**–$27
8–$20 **9**–$20

7 #156434

Robin
You Steal My Heart Away
Issued: 1996 • Current
Original Price: $17.50
Value by Year Mark:
5–$50 **6**–$30 **7**–$26
8–$17.50 **9**–$17.50

#203114

Balcony Display

Juliet

Romeo

T Is For Teddies

Sweetheart Collector Set (set/3, LE-1997)
Issued: 1997 • Closed: 1997
Original Price: $60
Value by Year Mark: **6**–$85 **7**–$75

② #158488A

Bear With A Block
Issued: 1995 • Current
Original Price: $5
Value: $5

③ #158488B

Bear With B Block
Issued: 1995 • Current
Original Price: $5
Value: $5

④ #158488C

Bear With C Block
Issued: 1995 • Current
Original Price: $5
Value: $5

⑤ #158488D

Bear With D Block
Issued: 1995 • Current
Original Price: $5
Value: $5

⑥ #158488E

Bear With E Block
Issued: 1995 • Current
Original Price: $5
Value: $5

SWEETHEART BALL

	Price Paid	Value Of My Collection
1.		

T IS FOR TEDDIES

2.		
3.		
4.		
5.		
6.		

PENCIL TOTALS

SWEETHEART/T IS

1   #158488F

Bear With F Block
Issued: 1995 • Current
Original Price: $5
Value: $5

2   #158488G

Bear With G Block
Issued: 1995 • Current
Original Price: $5
Value: $5

3   #158488H

Bear With H Block
Issued: 1995 • Current
Original Price: $5
Value: $5

4   #158488I

Bear With I Block
Issued: 1995 • Current
Original Price: $5
Value: $5

5   #158488J

Bear With J Block
Issued: 1995 • Current
Original Price: $5
Value: $5

6   #158488K

Bear With K Block
Issued: 1995 • Current
Original Price: $5
Value: $5

T Is For Teddies

	Price Paid	Value Of My Collection
1.		
2.		
3.		
4.		
5.		
6.		
7.		
8.		

PENCIL TOTALS

7   #158488L

Bear With L Block
Issued: 1995 • Current
Original Price: $5
Value: $5

8   #158488M

Bear With M Block
Issued: 1995 • Current
Original Price: $5
Value: $5

① #158488N

Bear With N Block
Issued: 1995 • Current
Original Price: $5
Value: $5

② #158488O

Bear With O Block
Issued: 1995 • Current
Original Price: $5
Value: $5

③ #158488P

Bear With P Block
Issued: 1995 • Current
Original Price: $5
Value: $5

④ #158488Q

Bear With Q Block
Issued: 1995 • Current
Original Price: $5
Value: $5

⑤ #158488R

Bear With R Block
Issued: 1995 • Current
Original Price: $5
Value: $5

⑥ #158488S

Bear With S Block
Issued: 1995 • Current
Original Price: $5
Value: $5

⑦ #158488T

Bear With T Block
Issued: 1995 • Current
Original Price: $5
Value: $5

⑧ #158488U

Bear With U Block
Issued: 1995 • Current
Original Price: $5
Value: $5

T IS FOR TEDDIES

	Price Paid	Value Of My Collection
1.		
2.		
3.		
4.		
5.		
6.		
7.		
8.		
PENCIL TOTALS		

(1) #158488V

Bear With V Block
Issued: 1995 • Current
Original Price: $5
Value: $5

(2) #158488W

Bear With W Block
Issued: 1995 • Current
Original Price: $5
Value: $5

(3) #158488X

Bear With X Block
Issued: 1995 • Current
Original Price: $5
Value: $5

(4) #158488Y

Bear With Y Block
Issued: 1995 • Current
Original Price: $5
Value: $5

(5) #158488Z

Bear With Z Block
Issued: 1995 • Current
Original Price: $5
Value: $5

Teddie Triumphs

T Is For Teddies

	Price Paid	Value Of My Collection
1.		
2.		
3.		
4.		
5.		

Teddie Triumphs

6.		
7.		

PENCIL TOTALS

(6) #477427

New!

Awesome!
Issued: 1999 • Current
Original Price: $7.50
Value: $7.50

(7) #477451

New!

Congratulations
Issued: 1999 • Current
Original Price: $7.50
Value: $7.50

① #477443
New!

Good Job
Issued: 1999 • Current
Original Price: $7.50
Value: $7.50

② #477478
New!

I'm Proud Of You
Issued: 1999 • Current
Original Price: $7.50
Value: $7.50

③ #477419
New!

Keep Trying
Issued: 1999 • Current
Original Price: $7.50
Value: $7.50

④ #477400
New!

You Did It
Issued: 1999 • Current
Original Price: $7.50
Value: $7.50

Teddies In Motion

⑤ #477524
New!

Chad
With You My Spirits Soar
Issued: 1999 • Current
Original Price: N/A
Value by Year Mark: **9**–N/E

⑥ #477494
New!

Dave
An Oldie But Goodie
Issued: 1999 • Current
Original Price: N/A
Value by Year Mark: **9**–N/E

⑦ #477508
New!

Dustin and Austin
(LE-1999)
*Hold On For The Ride
Of Your Life*
Issued: 1999
To Be Closed: 1999
Original Price: N/A
Value by Year Mark: **9**–N/E

TEDDIE TRIUMPHS

	Price Paid	Value Of My Collection
1.		
2.		
3.		
4.		

TEDDIES IN MOTION

5.		
6.		
7.		

PENCIL TOTALS

1 — #477559
New!

PHOTO UNAVAILABLE

Ken
You Make My Heart Race
Issued: 1999 • Current
Original Price: N/A
Value by Year Mark: **9**–N/E

2 — #477516
New!

PHOTO UNAVAILABLE

Roger
You Set My Heart In Motion
Issued: 1999 • Current
Original Price: N/A
Value by Year Mark: **9**–N/E

Through The Years

3 — #911348

Age 1
Beary Special One
Issued: 1993 • Current
Original Price: $13.50
Value by Year Mark:
LETTER–$37 **3**–$32 **4**–$29
5–$24 **6**–$16 **7**–$15
8–$13.50 **9**–$13.50

4 — #911321

Age 2
Two Sweet Two Bear
Issued: 1993 • Current
Original Price: $13.50
Value by Year Mark:
LETTER–$37 **3**–$32 **4**–$29
5–$24 **6**–$16 **7**–$15
8–$13.50 **9**–$13.50

5 — #911313

Age 3
Three Cheers For You
Issued: 1993 • Current
Original Price: $15
Value by Year Mark:
LETTER–$37 **3**–$32 **4**–$29
5–$24 **6**–$16 **7**–$15
8–$15 **9**–$15

TEDDIES IN MOTION

	Price Paid	Value Of My Collection
1.		
2.		

THROUGH THE YEARS

	Price Paid	Value Of My Collection
3.		
4.		
5.		
6.	15.00	32.00
7.		
	15.00	32.00

PENCIL TOTALS

6 — #911305

Age 4
Unfolding Happy Wishes Four You
Issued: 1993 • Current
Original Price: $15
Value by Year Mark:
LETTER–$37 **3**–$32 **4**–$29
5–$24 **6**–$16 **7**–$15
8–$15 **9**–$15

7 — #911291

Age 5
Color Me Five
Issued: 1993 • Current
Original Price: $15
Value by Year Mark:
LETTER–$37 **3**–$32 **4**–$29
5–$24 **6**–$16 **7**–$15
8–$15 **9**–$15

① #911283

Age 6
Chalking Up Six Wishes
Issued: 1993 • Current
Original Price: $16.50
Value by Year Mark:
LETTER–$39 **3**–$33 **4**–$30
5–$28 **6**–$22 **7**–$19
8–$16.50 **9**–$16.50
Variation: white elbow patch
with green dots
Value by Year Mark: **7**–$28

② #466239

Age 7
Seven Is As Sweet As Honey
Issued: 1998 • Current
Original Price: $16.50
Value by Year Mark:
8–$16.50 **9**–$16.50

③ #466247

Age 8
Being Eight Is Really Great!
Issued: 1998 • Current
Original Price: $16.50
Value by Year Mark:
8–$16.50 **9**–$16.50

④ #466255

Age 9
Being Nine Is Really Fine!
Issued: 1998 • Current
Original Price: $16.50
Value by Year Mark:
8–$16.50 **9**–$16.50

⑤ #466263

Age 10
Count To Ten . . . And Celebrate!
Issued: 1998 • Current
Original Price: $16.50
Value by Year Mark:
8–$16.50 **9**–$16.50

⑥ #911356

Baby
Cradled With Love
Issued: 1993 • Current
Original Price: $16.50
Value by Year Mark:
LETTER–$39 **3**–$33 **4**–$30
5–$28 **6**–$22 **7**–$19
8–$16.50 **9**–$16.50

Up In The Attic

⑦ #302600

Kaitlyn (LE-1998)
Old Treasures, New Memories
Issued: 1998 • Closed: 1998
Original Price: $50
Value by Year Mark: **8**–$56

THROUGH THE YEARS

	Price Paid	Value Of My Collection
1.		
2.		
3.		
4.		
5.		
6.		

UP IN THE ATTIC

7.		

PENCIL TOTALS

THROUGH THE/UP IN

① #308684

Future Release!

Lauren (LE-2000)
Cherished Memories Never Fade
To Be Issued: 2000
Original Price: $35
Value by Year Mark: N/E

② #308676

New!

Sarah (LE-1999)
Memories To Wear And Share
Issued: 1999
To Be Closed: 1999
Original Price: $30
Value by Year Mark: **9**–$30

We Bear Thanks

③ #141305

Barbara
Giving Thanks For Our Family
Issued: 1996 • Retired: 1997
Original Price: $12.50
Value by Year Mark:
6–$26 **7**–$19

④ #141275

Dina
Bear In Mind, You're Special
Issued: 1996 • Retired: 1997
Original Price: $15
Value by Year Mark:
6–$30 **7**–$22

⑤ #141283

John
Bear In Mind, You're Special
Issued: 1996 • Retired: 1997
Original Price: $15
Value by Year Mark:
6–$30 **7**–$22

UP IN THE ATTIC

	Price Paid	Value Of My Collection
1.		
2.		

WE BEAR THANKS

3.		
4.		
5.		
6.		
7.		

PENCIL TOTALS

⑥ #141291

Rick
Suited Up For The Holidays
Issued: 1996 • Retired: 1997
Original Price: $12.50
Value by Year Mark:
6–$26 **7**–$19

⑦ #141542

Table With Food And Dog
Issued: 1996 • Retired: 1997
Original Price: $30
Value by Year Mark:
6–$52 **7**–$42

① #175560

Displayer
Barbara
Rick
Dina
Table With Food And Dog
John

We Bear Thanks Collector Set (set/6)
Issued: 1996 • Current
Original Price: $85
Value by Year Mark: **6**–$164 **7**–$124

Winter Bear Festival

---

② #269751

Adam
It's A Holiday On Ice
Issued: 1997 • Current
Original Price: $20
Value by Year Mark:
7–$27 **8**–$20 **9**–$20

③ #269778

Candace
Skating On Holiday Joy
Issued: 1997 • Current
Original Price: $20
Value by Year Mark:
7–$28 **8**–$20 **9**–$20

④ #292575

Festival Boy Musical Waterglobe
♪ *White Christmas*
Issued: 1997
Out Of Production: 1998
Original Price: $45
Value: $50

---

⑤ #272884

Festival Girl Musical Waterglobe
♪ *Let It Snow*
Issued: 1997
Out Of Production: 1998
Original Price: $45
Value: $50

⑥ #269786

James
Going My Way For The Holidays
Issued: 1997 • Current
Original Price: $25
Value by Year Mark:
7–$34 **8**–$25 **9**–$25

WE BEAR THANKS	Price Paid	Value Of My Collection
1.		

WINTER BEAR FESTIVAL		
2.		
3.		
4.		
5.		
6.		
PENCIL TOTALS		

① #141178

Lindsey and Lyndon
Walking In A Winter Wonderland
Issued: 1997 • Current
Original Price: $30
Value by Year Mark:
7–$36 **8**–$30 **9**–$30

② #141178A

Lindsey and Lyndon
(1996 Catalog Exclusive)
Walking In A Winter Wonderland
Issued: 1996 • Closed: 1996
Original Price: $30
Value by Year Mark: **6**–$72

③ #269735

Mitch
Friendship Never Melts Away
Issued: 1997 • Current
Original Price: $30
Value by Year Mark:
7–$38 **8**–$30 **9**–$30

④ #269743

Spencer
I'm Head Over Skis For You
Issued: 1997 • Current
Original Price: $20
Value by Year Mark:
7–$28 **8**–$20 **9**–$20

⑤ #269727

Ted
*Snow Fun When You're
Not Around*
Issued: 1997 • Current
Original Price: $18.50
Value by Year Mark:
7–$23 **8**–$18.50 **9**–$18.50

WINTER BEAR FESTIVAL

	Price Paid	Value Of My Collection
1.		
2.		
3.	30.00	38.00
4.	20.00	28.00
5.		
	50.00	66.00

PENCIL TOTALS

OTHER COLLECTIBLES

Throughout the years, an assortment of almost 200 pieces featuring **Cherished Teddies** designs has appeared on bells, bookends, candleholders, clocks, eggs, frames, lamps, musicals, ornaments, plaques, plates and stocking holders. Each of these collectibles is listed in this section in alphabetical order by product type. In the Spring of 1999, 17 new pieces were added to the collection.

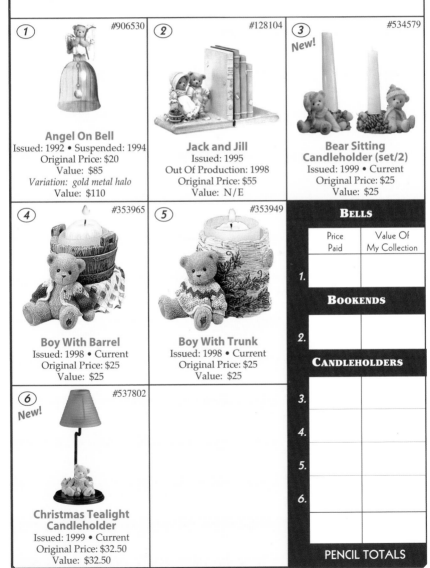

① #906530

Angel On Bell
Issued: 1992 • Suspended: 1994
Original Price: $20
Value: $85
Variation: gold metal halo
Value: $110

② #128104

Jack and Jill
Issued: 1995
Out Of Production: 1998
Original Price: $55
Value: N/E

③ New! #534579

**Bear Sitting
Candleholder (set/2)**
Issued: 1999 • Current
Original Price: $25
Value: $25

④ #353965

Boy With Barrel
Issued: 1998 • Current
Original Price: $25
Value: $25

⑤ #353949

Boy With Trunk
Issued: 1998 • Current
Original Price: $25
Value: $25

⑥ New! #537802

**Christmas Tealight
Candleholder**
Issued: 1999 • Current
Original Price: $32.50
Value: $32.50

BELLS/BOOKENDS/CANDLE

	Price Paid	Value Of My Collection
BELLS		
1.		
BOOKENDS		
2.		
CANDLEHOLDERS		
3.		
4.		
5.		
6.		
PENCIL TOTALS		

(1) #353922

Girl With Basket
Issued: 1998 • Current
Original Price: $25
Value: $25

(2) #353914

Girl With Blanket
Issued: 1998 • Current
Original Price: $25
Value: $25

(3) #353957

Girl With Pinecones
Issued: 1998 • Current
Original Price: $25
Value: $25

(4) #353973

Girl With Tree Trunk
Issued: 1998 • Current
Original Price: $25
Value: $25

(5) #132993

Jack and Jill
Issued: 1995
Out Of Production: 1997
Original Price: $50
Value: N/E

(6) #156604

Our Cherished Family
Issued: 1996
Out Of Production: 1998
Original Price: $50
Value: N/E

CANDLEHOLDERS	Price Paid	Value Of My Collection
1.		
2.		
3.		
4.		
CLOCKS		
5.		
• 6.		
7.		
8.		
EGGS		
9.		
10.		
PENCIL TOTALS		

(7) #203939

Rock-A-Bye Baby
Issued: 1997 • Current
Original Price: $55
Value: $55

(8) #132977

Tea Time
Issued: 1995
Out Of Production: 1998
Original Price: $50
Value: N/E

(9) #476951
New!

Easter Eggs (3 asst.)
Egg With Green Bow
Issued: 1999 • Current
Original Price: $10
Value: $10

(10) #476951
New!

Easter Eggs (3 asst.)
Egg With Pink Bow
Issued: 1999 • Current
Original Price: $10
Value: $10

(1) New! #476951

Easter Eggs (3 asst.)
Egg With Yellow Bow
Issued: 1999 • Current
Original Price: $10
Value: $10

(2) #156507

Easter (Dated 1996)
Issued: 1996 • Closed: 1996
Original Price: $8.50
Value: $17

(3) #203017

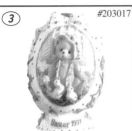

Easter (Dated 1997)
Issued: 1997 • Closed: 1997
Original Price: $10
Value: $14

(4) #203920

Baby
Issued: 1997 • Current
Original Price: $22.50
Value: $22.50

(5) #203882

Baby & Me
Issued: 1997
Out Of Production: 1998
Original Price: $22.50
Value: N/E

(6) #912999

Bear With Scarf
Issued: 1993
Out Of Production: 1996
Original Price: $20
Value: $35

(7) #910791

**Boy And Girl
(double heart frame)**
Issued: 1993
Out Of Production: 1996
Original Price: $27.50
Value: $82

(8) #911704

**Boy And Girl
(double oval frame)**
Issued: 1994
Out Of Production: 1997
Original Price: $30
Value: $52

(9) #911720

Boy Praying
Issued: 1993 • Current
Original Price: $20
Value: $20

(10) #902772

Boy Sailor
Issued: 1993
Out Of Production: 1997
Original Price: $20
Value: $28

	EGGS	
	Price Paid	Value Of My Collection
1.		
2.		
3.		
	FRAMES	
4.		
5.		
6.		
7.		
8.		
9.		
10.		
	PENCIL TOTALS	

EGGS/FRAMES

131

① #910783

Boy With Cat
Issued: 1993
Out Of Production: 1993
Original Price: $19.50
Value: $50

② #104191

Boy With Puppy
Issued: 1995 • Current
Original Price: $20
Value: $20

③ #906700

Boy With Santa Cap
Issued: 1992
Out Of Production: 1995
Original Price: $20
Value: $55

④ #627364

**Bride And Groom
(invitation holder)**
Issued: 1994 • Current
Original Price: $37.50
Value: $37.50

⑤ #128074

Daddy And Me
Issued: 1996 • Current
Original Price: $25
Value: $25

⑥ #906700

Girl In Stocking
Issued: 1992
Out Of Production: 1995
Original Price: $20
Value: $43

	Price Paid	Value Of My Collection
1.		
2.		
3.		
4.		
5.		
6.		
7.		
8.		
9.		
10.		

FRAMES

PENCIL TOTALS

⑦ #911712

Girl Praying
Issued: 1993 • Current
Original Price: $20
Value: $20

⑧ #136182

Girl Reading With Doll
Issued: 1995 • Current
Original Price: $20
Value: $20

⑨ #902772

Girl Sailor
Issued: 1993
Out Of Production: 1997
Original Price: $20
Value: $28

⑩ #912999

Girl With Doll
Issued: 1993
Out Of Production: 1996
Original Price: $20
Value: $36

① #910783

Girl With Hearts
Issued: 1993
Out Of Production: 1993
Original Price: $19.50
Value: $44

② #128112

Jack and Jill
Issued: 1995
Out Of Production: 1997
Original Price: $30
Value: $40

③ #128066

Mommy And Me
Issued: 1996 • Current
Original Price: $25
Value: $25

④ #128082

My Buddy And Me
Issued: 1996
Out Of Production: 1998
Original Price: $25
Value: N/E

⑤ #128120

My Cherished Family
Issued: 1995 • Current
Original Price: $25
Value: $25

⑥ #136174

My Cherished Friend
Issued: 1995
Out Of Production: 1996
Original Price: $25
Value: $35

⑦ #136166

My Cherished Grandma
Issued: 1995
Out Of Production: 1996
Original Price: $25
Value: $35

⑧ #135755

My Cherished Mom
Issued: 1995
Out Of Production: 1996
Original Price: $25
Value: $35

⑨ #103691

My Cherished One
Issued: 1995
Out Of Production: 1996
Original Price: $25
Value: $35

⑩ #617210

My Visit To Santa
Issued: 1994 • Current
Original Price: $20
Value: $20

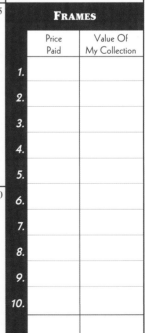

FRAMES

	Price Paid	Value Of My Collection
1.		
2.		
3.		
4.		
5.		
6.		
7.		
8.		
9.		
10.		
	PENCIL TOTALS	

FRAMES

① #624934

**Our Bundle Of Joy
(birth record)**
Issued: 1994 • Current
Original Price: $20
Value: $20

② #476838

New!

Wedding Photo Frame
Issued: 1999 • Current
Original Price: $30
Value: $30

③ #311588

January
January is a garnet,
strong and bold.
Like a friend
who has a heart
of gold!

**Bear With January
Birthstone**
Issued: 1998 • Current
Original Price: $12.50
Value: $12.50

④ #311596

February
February – an amethyst
patient and true.
Sharing the
blessings of
friendship for
you!

**Bear With February
Birthstone**
Issued: 1998 • Current
Original Price: $12.50
Value: $12.50

⑤ #311618

March
March sets sail with an
aquamarine to find.
A forever friend
who's understanding
and kind!

**Bear With March
Birthstone**
Issued: 1998 • Current
Original Price: $12.50
Value: $12.50

⑥ #311626

April
April showers
sent from above.
Make diamonds
sparkle with
tender love!

**Bear With April
Birthstone**
Issued: 1998 • Current
Original Price: $12.50
Value: $12.50

FRAMES

	Price Paid	Value Of My Collection
1.		
2.		

**LITTLE SPARKLES
– FRAMES –**

3.		
4.		
5.	12.50	12.50
6.		
7.		
8.		
9.		
10.		
	12.50	12.50

PENCIL TOTALS

⑦ #311634

May
May is an emerald
kind and sincere.
A gift of friendship
a treasure
so dear!

**Bear With May
Birthstone**
Issued: 1998 • Current
Original Price: $12.50
Value: $12.50

⑧ #311642

June
June is a alexandrite,
the heart of love.
Expressing
friendship sent
from above!

**Bear With June
Birthstone**
Issued: 1998 • Current
Original Price: $12.50
Value: $12.50

⑨ #311650

July
July is a ruby,
shining so bright;
filled with wonder,
joy and delight!

**Bear With July
Birthstone**
Issued: 1998 • Current
Original Price: $12.50
Value: $12.50

⑩ #311669

August
August – a peridot
gemstone for you.
Filled with pride
and honor
so true.

**Bear With August
Birthstone**
Issued: 1998 • Current
Original Price: $12.50
Value: $12.50

① #311677

Bear With September Birthstone
Issued: 1998 • Current
Original Price: $12.50
Value: $12.50

② #311707

Bear With October Birthstone
Issued: 1998 • Current
Original Price: $12.50
Value: $12.50

③ #311715

Bear With November Birthstone
Issued: 1998 • Current
Original Price: $12.50
Value: $12.50

④ #311723

Bear With December Birthstone
Issued: 1998 • Current
Original Price: $12.50
Value: $12.50

⑤ #139114

Bear Holding Heart
Issued: 1995
Out Of Production: 1997
Original Price: $100
Value: $110

⑥ #912425

Theodore, Samantha and Tyler
Issued: 1993
Out Of Production: 1995
Original Price: $175
Value: $190

⑦ #699314

Baby Boy (jointed)
♪ *Schubert's Lullaby*
Issued: 1994 • Suspended: 1997
Out Of Production: 1998
Original Price: $60
Value: $72

⑧ #699322

Baby Girl (jointed)
♪ *Schubert's Lullaby*
Issued: 1994 • Suspended: 1997
Out Of Production: 1998
Original Price: $60
Value: $72

⑨ #914320

Baby In Cradle
♪ *Brahms' Lullaby*
Issued: 1993 • Current
Original Price: $60
Value: $60

⑩ #331473

Bear Ballerina
♪ *Music Box Dancer*
Issued: 1998 • Current
Original Price: $40
Value: $40

FRAMES/LAMPS/MUSICALS

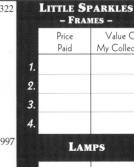

	Price Paid	Value Of My Collection
LITTLE SPARKLES – FRAMES –		
1.		
2.		
3.		
4.		
LAMPS		
5.		
6.		
MUSICALS		
7.		
8.		
9.		
10.		
PENCIL TOTALS		

① #625302

Bear In Bunny Hat (jointed)
♪ *Here Comes Peter Cottontail*
Issued: 1994 • Retired: 1996
Original Price: $60
Value: $86

② #950785

Bear In Stocking Cap (waterdome)
♪ *Have Yourself A Merry Little Christmas*
Issued: 1992 • Suspended: 1995
Original Price: $60
Value: $120

③ #331457

Bear In Teacup
♪ *My Favorite Things*
Issued: 1998 • Current
Original Price: $40
Value: $40

④ #331465

Bear In Train
♪ *Toyland*
Issued: 1998 • Current
Original Price: $40
Value: $40

⑤ #900354

Bear On Rocking Reindeer (waterdome)
♪ *Let It Snow*
Issued: 1992 • Suspended: 1994
Original Price: $60
Value: $115

⑥ #912964

Bear With Toy Train
♪ *Santa Claus Is Coming To Town*
Issued: 1993 • Current
Original Price: $40
Value: $40

MUSICALS

	Price Paid	Value Of My Collection
1.		
2.		
3.		
4.		
5.		
6.		
7.		
8.		
9.		
10.		
PENCIL TOTALS		

⑦ #914304

Boy Praying
♪ *Jesus Loves Me*
Issued: 1993 • Retired: 1997
Original Price: $37.50
Value: $65

⑧ #699349

Bride And Groom
♪ *Mendelssohn Wedding March*
Issued: 1994 • Current
Original Price: $50
Value: $50

⑨ #912859

Cherish The King
♪ *O Little Town Of Bethlehem*
Issued: 1993 • Suspended: 1995
Original Price: $60
Value: $100

⑩ #903337

Christmas Bear (jointed)
♪ *Jingle Bells*
Issued: 1993 • Suspended: 1995
Original Price: $60
Value: $95

① #336459

Clown On Ball
♪ *You Are My Sunshine*
Issued: 1998 • Current
Original Price: $40
Value: $40

② #624926

Couple In Laundry Basket
♪ *Love Will Keep Us Together*
Issued: 1994 • Current
Original Price: $60
Value: $60

③ #651435

Couple In Sleigh
♪ *Oh, What A Merry Christmas Day*
Issued: 1994
Out Of Production: 1998
Original Price: $100
Value: N/E

④ #904546

Family On Toboggan
♪ *Jingle Bells*
Issued: 1993 • Suspended: 1995
Original Price: $170
Value: $260

⑤ #128058

Girl On Ottoman
♪ *Au Claire De La Lune*
Issued: 1995 • Current
Original Price: $55
Value: $55

⑥ #628565

Girl On Rocking Horse
♪ *My Favorite Things*
Issued: 1994 • Retired: 1996
Original Price: $150
Value: $190

⑦ #629618

**Girl On Rocking
Reindeer (12.5")**
♪ *Jingle Bells*
Issued: 1994
Out Of Production: 1998
Original Price: $165
Value: N/E

⑧ #950815

**Girl On Rocking
Reindeer (6")**
♪ *Jingle Bells*
Issued: 1992 • Suspended: 1994
Original Price: $60
Value: $150

⑨ #914312

Girl Praying
♪ *Jesus Loves Me*
Issued: 1993 • Retired: 1997
Original Price: $37.50
Value: $62

⑩ #627445

Girl With Goose
♪ *Wind Beneath My Wings*
Issued: 1994 • Retired: 1997
Original Price: $45
Value: $78

MUSICALS

	Price Paid	Value Of My Collection
1.		
2.		
3.		
4.		
5.		
6.		
7.		
8.		
9.		
10.		
PENCIL TOTALS		

MUSICALS

① #916323

Girl With Heart Harp
♪ *Love Makes The World Go Round*
Issued: 1994 • Retired: 1997
Original Price: $40
Value: $65

② #903779

Girl With Muff (waterdome)
♪ *White Christmas*
Issued: 1993 • Suspended: 1995
Original Price: $50
Value: $110

③ #950645

Girls In Basket With Umbrella
♪ *Let Me Be Your Teddy Bear*
Issued: 1992 • Retired: 1997
Original Price: $60
Value: $85

④ #627453

Teddie With Toy Chest
♪ *My Favorite Things*
Issued: 1994 • Current
Original Price: $60
Value: $60

⑤ #141089

Two Boys By Lamppost
♪ *The First Noel*
Issued: 1996 • Current
Original Price: $50
Value: $50

⑥ #476900

New!

Wedding Action Musical
♪ *Mendelssohn Wedding March*
Issued: 1999 • Current
Original Price: $40
Value: $40

MUSICALS

	Price Paid	Value Of My Collection
1.		
2.		
3.		
4.		
5.		
6.		

ORNAMENTS

7.		
8.		
9.		
10.		

PENCIL TOTALS

⑦ #950777

Angel
Issued: 1992 • Suspended: 1994
Original Price: $12.50
Value: $70
Variation: gold metal halo
Value: $90

⑧ #141240

Baby Angel On Cloud
Issued: 1995 • Current
Original Price: $13.50
Value: $13.50

⑨ #617253

Baby In Basket (Dated 1994)
Issued: 1994 • Closed: 1994
Original Price: $15
Value: $42

⑩ #913014

Baby's First Christmas (Dated 1993)
Issued: 1993 • Closed: 1993
Original Price: $12.50
Value: $40

(1) #913006

Baby's First Christmas (Dated 1993)
Issued: 1993 • Closed: 1993
Original Price: $12.50
Value: $40

(2) #914894

Bear In Santa Cap (jointed)
Issued: 1993 • Suspended: 1995
Original Price: $12.50
Value: $36

(3) #950653

Bear In Stocking (Dated 1992)
Issued: 1992 • Closed: 1992
Original Price: $16
Value: $60

(4) #950793

Bear On Rocking Reindeer
Issued: 1992 • Suspended: 1994
Original Price: $20
Value: $63

(5) New! #537004

Bear With Blue Hat/Scarf
Issued: 1999 • Current
Original Price: $7.50
Value: $7.50

(6) #177768

Bear With Dangling Mittens
Issued: 1996 • Current
Original Price: $12.50
Value: $12.50

(7) New! #537004

Bear With Green Hat/Scarf
Issued: 1999 • Current
Original Price: $7.50
Value: $7.50

(8) #141232

Bear With Ice Skates (Dated 1995)
Issued: 1995 • Closed: 1995
Original Price: $12.50
Value: $42

(9) New! #537004

Bear With Red Hat/Scarf
Issued: 1999 • Current
Original Price: $7.50
Value: $7.50

(10) #141259

Boy And Girl With Banner
Issued: 1995 • Current
Original Price: $13.50
Value: $13.50

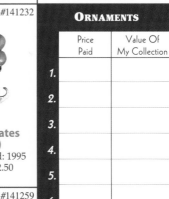

	ORNAMENTS	
	Price Paid	Value Of My Collection
1.		
2.		
3.		
4.		
5.		
6.		
7.		
8.	12.50	42.00
9.		
10.		
	12.50	42.00
PENCIL TOTALS		

ORNAMENTS

① #617229

Cherished Teddies In Sleigh (Dated 1994)
Issued: 1994 • Closed: 1994
Original Price: $15
Value: $38

② #354090

Christmas Advent Calendar
Issued: 1998 • Current
Original Price: $50
Value: $50

③ #272175

Dangling Snow Flake (Dated 1997)
Issued: 1997 • Closed: 1997
Original Price: $12.50
Value: $23

④ #912891

Drummer Boy (Dated 1994)
Issued: 1994 • Closed: 1994
Original Price: $10
Value: $42

⑤ #534161
New!

Eskimo Holding Fish (set/2, Dated 1999 & 2000)
Issued: 1999
To Be Closed: 1999
Original Price: $25
Value: $25

⑥ #352748

Gingerbread Bear (Dated 1998)
Issued: 1998 • Closed: 1998
Original Price: $12.50
Value: $18

ORNAMENTS

	Price Paid	Value Of My Collection
1.		
2.		
3.	12.50	2300
4.	10.00	42.00
5.		
6.		
7.		
8.		
9.		
10.		
	22.50	65.00

PENCIL TOTALS

⑦ #912832

Girl With Muff (Dated 1993)
Issued: 1993 • Closed: 1993
Original Price: $13.50
Value: $58

⑧ #103608

Sending You My Heart
Issued: 1995 • Suspended: 1995
Original Price: $13
Value: $30

⑨ #103616

Sending You My Heart
Issued: 1995 • Suspended: 1995
Original Price: $13
Value: $30

⑩ #951226

Sister With Boots (mini)
Issued: 1992 • Suspended: 1995
Original Price: $12.50
Value: $32

(1) #951226

Sister With Bow (mini)
Issued: 1992 • Suspended: 1995
Original Price: $12.50
Value: $32

(2) #951226

Sister With Scarf (mini)
Issued: 1992 • Suspended: 1995
Original Price: $12.50
Value: $32

(3) #176052

**Toy Soldier
(Dated 1996)**
Issued: 1996 • Closed: 1996
Original Price: $12.50
Value: $28

(4) #451010

American Boy
Issued: 1998 • Current
Original Price: $10
Value: $10

(5) #464120

Australian Boy
Issued: 1998 • Current
Original Price: $10
Value: $10

(6) #451053

Canadian Boy
Issued: 1998 • Current
Original Price: $10
Value: $10

(7) #450960

Chinese Boy
Issued: 1998 • Current
Original Price: $10
Value: $10

(8) #450995

Dutch Girl
Issued: 1998 • Current
Original Price: $10
Value: $10

(9) #451045

English Boy
Issued: 1998 • Current
Original Price: $10
Value: $10

(10) #450901

French Girl
Issued: 1998 • Current
Original Price: $10
Value: $10

ORNAMENTS

	Price Paid	Value Of My Collection
1.		
2.		
3.	12.50	28.00

**ACROSS THE SEAS
– ORNAMENTS –**

4.		
5.		
6.		
7.		
8.		
9.		
10.		
	12.50	28.00

PENCIL TOTALS

ORNAMENTS

① #451002  **German Boy** Issued: 1998 • Current Original Price: $10 Value: $10	② #450987  **Indian Girl** Issued: 1998 • Current Original Price: $10 Value: $10	③ #464112  **Italian Girl** Issued: 1998 • Current Original Price: $10 Value: $10
④ #450936  **Japanese Girl** Issued: 1998 • Current Original Price: $10 Value: $10	⑤ #450952  **Mexican Boy** Issued: 1998 • Current Original Price: $10 Value: $10	⑥ #450944  **Russian Girl** Issued: 1998 • Current Original Price: $10 Value: $10

ACROSS THE SEAS
– ORNAMENTS –

	Price Paid	Value Of My Collection
1.		
2.		
3.		
4.		
5.		
6.		
7.		
8.		
9.		

PLAQUES

10.		

PENCIL TOTALS

⑦ #451029
Scottish Girl
Issued: 1998 • Current
Original Price: $10
Value: $10

⑧ #450979
Spanish Boy
Issued: 1998 • Current
Original Price: $10
Value: $10

⑨ #450928
Swedish Girl
Issued: 1998 • Current
Original Price: $10
Value: $10

⑩ #203718
Baby
Issued: 1997
Out Of Production: 1998
Original Price: $27.50
Value: $27.50

① #482064

New!

Baby Girl With Lamb
Issued: 1999 • Current
Original Price: $10
Value: $10

② #534668

New!

Bear In Hat And Scarf (mini)
Issued: 1999 • Current
Original Price: $12
Value: $12

③ #534668

New!

Bear In Santa Suit (mini)
Issued: 1999 • Current
Original Price: $12
Value: $12

④ #534668

New!

Bear With Puppy (mini)
Issued: 1999 • Current
Original Price: $12
Value: $12

⑤ #203211

Bears With Double Hearts
Love Bears All Things
Issued: 1997 • Current
Original Price: $15
Value: $15

⑥ #482064

New!

Birthday Bear
Issued: 1999 • Current
Original Price: $10
Value: $10

⑦ #482064

New!

Boy Graduate
Issued: 1999 • Current
Original Price: $10
Value: $10

⑧ #482064

New!

Bride And Groom
Issued: 1999 • Current
Original Price: $10
Value: $10

⑨ #104140

Charity
Issued: 1995 • Current
Original Price: $10
Value: $10

⑩ #110981

A Cherished Irish Blessing
Issued: 1995 • Suspended: 1995
Out Of Production: 1998
Original Price: $13.50
Value: N/E

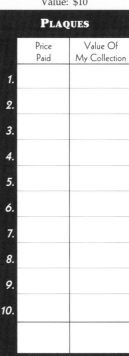

PLAQUES

	Price Paid	Value Of My Collection
1.		
2.		
3.		
4.		
5.		
6.		
7.		
8.		
9.		
10.		
	PENCIL TOTALS	

PLAQUES

① #104140  **Faith** Issued: 1995 • Current Original Price: $10 Value: $10	**②** #627372  **A Friend Is A Treasure Of The Heart** Issued: 1994 • Current Original Price: $10 Value: $10	**③** #104116 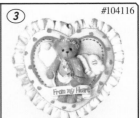 **From My Heart** Issued: 1995 Out Of Production: 1997 Original Price: $10 Value: $18

④ #482064 New!  **Girl And Boy With Kite** Issued: 1999 • Current Original Price: $10 Value: $10	**⑤** #482064 New! **Girls With Teddies And Cookies** Issued: 1999 • Current Original Price: $10 Value: $10	**⑥** #104116  **Heart To Heart** Issued: 1995 Out Of Production: 1997 Original Price: $10 Value: $18

PLAQUES

	Price Paid	Value Of My Collection
1.	10.00	10.00
2.		
3.		
4.		
5.		
6.		
7.		
8.		
9.		
10.		

PENCIL TOTALS

⑦ #303186  **Heaven Has Blessed This Day** Issued: 1998 • Current Original Price: $10 Value: $10	**⑧** #303186 **Heaven Has Blessed This Day** Issued: 1998 • Current Original Price: $10 Value: $10
⑨ #303208  **Heaven Has Blessed This Day** Issued: 1998 • Current Original Price: $17.50 Value: $17.50	**⑩** #303208  **Heaven Has Blessed This Day** Issued: 1998 • Current Original Price: $17.50 Value: $17.50

① #627372

Home Is Where The Heart Is
Issued: 1994 • Current
Original Price: $10
Value: $10

② #104140

Hope
Issued: 1995 • Current
Original Price: $10
Value: $10

③ #627372

Live Well, Laugh Often, Love Much
Issued: 1994 • Current
Original Price: $10
Value: $10

④ #104140

Love
Issued: 1995 • Current
Original Price: $10
Value: $10

⑤ #303054

Mom – Maker Of Miracles
Issued: 1998 • Current
Original Price: $15
Value: $15

⑥ #104116

My Cherished One
Issued: 1995
Out Of Production: 1997
Original Price: $10
Value: $18

⑦ #951005

Signage Plaque
Issued: 1992 • Current
Original Price: $15
Value: $15
Variation: "Hamilton" on front and understamp
Value: $90
Variation: "Enesco" on front, "Hamilton" on understamp
Value: $100

⑧ #203742

Sweet Little One Cross
Issued: 1997 • Current
Original Price: $15
Value: $15

⑨ #651427

We Bear Thanks
Issued: 1994 • Current
Original Price: $13.50
Value: $13.50

⑩ #627372

Welcome
Issued: 1994 • Current
Original Price: $10
Value: $10

PLAQUES

	Price Paid	Value Of My Collection
1.		
2.	10.00	10.00
3.		
4.	10.00	10.00
5.		
6.	10.00	18.00
7.		
8.		
9.		
10.		
	30.00	38.00
PENCIL TOTALS		

PLAQUES

① #176303

Angel In Red Coat
The Season Of Peace
Issued: 1996
Out Of Production: 1998
Original Price: $12.50
Value: N/E

② #176346

Baby's First Christmas
Issued: 1996
Out Of Production: 1998
Original Price: $12.50
Value: N/E

③ #176117

Girl In Red Coat
The Season Of Love
Issued: 1996
Out Of Production: 1998
Original Price: $12.50
Value: N/E

④ #176281

Girl With Green Coat
The Season Of Joy
Issued: 1996
Out Of Production: 1998
Original Price: $12.50
Value: N/E

⑤ #176311

Our First Christmas
Our First Christmas Together
Issued: 1996
Out Of Production: 1998
Original Price: $12.50
Value: N/E

⑥ #176338

**Santa With Tree
And Toys**
The Season For Santa
Issued: 1996
Out Of Production: 1998
Original Price: $12.50
Value: N/E

**TIS THE SEASON
– PLAQUES –**

	Price Paid	Value Of My Collection
1.		
2.		
3.		
4.	12.50	N/E
5.		
6.	12.50	N/E

PLATES

7.		
8.		
9.		
10.		
	25.00	N/E

PENCIL TOTALS

⑦ #156590

Easter (Dated 1996)
Some Bunny Loves You
Issued: 1996 • Closed: 1996
Original Price: $35
Value: $50

⑧ #203009

Easter (Dated 1997)
Springtime Happiness
Issued: 1997 • Closed: 1997
Original Price: $35
Value: $48

⑨ #534196

New!

**Eskimos Holding Stars
(Dated 1999 & 2000)**
Issued: 1999
To Be Closed: 1999
Original Price: $37.50
Value: $37.50

⑩ #303046

Mom – Maker Of Miracles
Issued: 1998
Out Of Production: 1998
Original Price: $35
Value: N/E

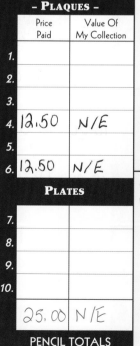

1 #156493

**Mother's Day
(Dated 1996)**
A Mother's Heart Is Full Of Love
Issued: 1996 • Closed: 1996
Original Price: $35
Value: $47

2 #203025

**Mother's Day
(Dated 1997)**
Our Love Is Ever-blooming
Issued: 1997 • Closed: 1997
Original Price: $35
Value: $45

3 #141550

**The Season Of Joy
(Dated 1995)**
Issued: 1995 • Closed: 1995
Original Price: $35
Value: $48

4 #352764

**The Season Of Magic
(Dated 1998)**
Issued: 1998 • Closed: 1998
Original Price: $35
Value: $40

5 #176060

**The Season Of Peace
(Dated 1996)**
Issued: 1996 • Closed: 1996
Original Price: $35
Value: $50

6 #272183

**The Season To Believe
(Dated 1997)**
Issued: 1997 • Closed: 1997
Original Price: $35
Value: $45

7 #203726

Sweet Little One
Issued: 1997
Out Of Production: 1998
Original Price: $35
Value: N/E

8 #272426

We Bear Thanks
Issued: 1997
Out Of Production: 1998
Original Price: $35
Value: N/E

9 #203408

**Autumn Brings A Season
Of Thanksgiving**
Issued: 1997 • Current
Original Price: $35
Value: $35

10 #203386

**Spring Brings A
Season Of Beauty**
Issued: 1997 • Current
Original Price: $35
Value: $35

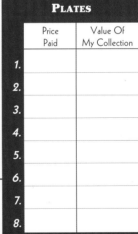

PLATES

	Price Paid	Value Of My Collection
1.		
2.		
3.		
4.		
5.		
6.		
7.		
8.		

**THE CHERISHED SEASONS
– PLATES –**

9.		
10.		

PENCIL TOTALS

PLATES

① #203394

Summer Brings A Season Of Warmth
Issued: 1997 • Current
Original Price: $35
Value: $35

② #203416

Winter Brings A Season Of Joy
Issued: 1997 • Current
Original Price: $35
Value: $35

③ #114901

Jack and Jill
Our Friendship Will Never Tumble
Issued: 1995
Out Of Production: 1998
Original Price: $35
Value: N/E

④ #164658

Little Bo Peep
Looking For A Friend Like You
Issued: 1996Out Of Production: 1998
Original Price: $35
Value: N/E

⑤ #151998

Little Jack Horner
I'm Plum Happy You're My Friend
Issued: 1996Out Of Production: 1998
Original Price: $35
Value: N/E

⑥ #145033

Little Miss Muffet
I'm Never Afraid With You At My Side
Issued: 1996Out Of Production: 1998
Original Price: $35
Value: N/E

THE CHERISHED SEASONS – PLATES –

	Price Paid	Value Of My Collection
1.		
2.		

NURSERY RHYME PLATES

3.		
4.		
5.		
6.		
7.		
8.		
9.		
10.		

PENCIL TOTALS

⑦ #128902

Mary Had A Little Lamb
I'll Always Be By Your Side
Issued: 1995
Out Of Production: 1998
Original Price: $35
Value: N/E

⑧ #170968

Mother Goose And Friends
Happily Ever After With Friends
Issued: 1996
Out Of Production: 1998
Original Price: $35
Value: N/E

⑨ #135437

Old King Cole
You Wear Your Kindness Like A Crown
Issued: 1995
Out Of Production: 1998
Original Price: $35
Value: N/E

⑩ #170941

Wee Willie Winkie
Good Night, Sleep Tight
Issued: 1996
Out Of Production: 1998
Original Price: $35
Value: N/E

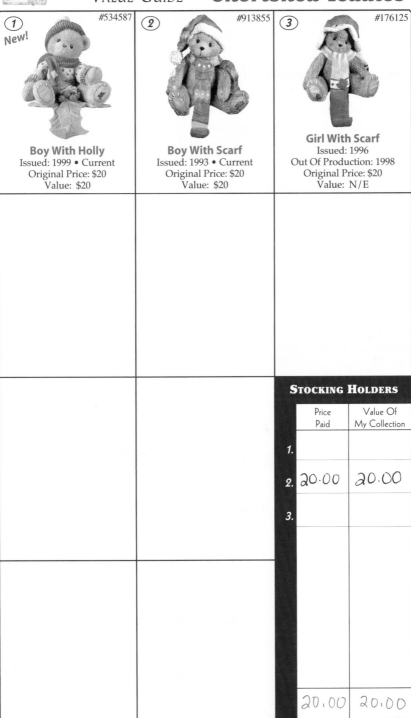

① #534587

New!

Boy With Holly
Issued: 1999 • Current
Original Price: $20
Value: $20

② #913855

Boy With Scarf
Issued: 1993 • Current
Original Price: $20
Value: $20

③ #176125

Girl With Scarf
Issued: 1996
Out Of Production: 1998
Original Price: $20
Value: N/E

STOCKING HOLDERS

	Price Paid	Value Of My Collection
1.		
2.	20.00	20.00
3.		
	20.00	20.00

PENCIL TOTALS

STOCKING HOLDERS

PLUSH

In 1993, seven plush pieces were introduced into the **Cherished Teddies** line with "Elsa" in small, medium and large versions and "Norman" in small, medium, large and a musical version. "Christmas Bear" made his debut in 1994 and then in 1995, a musical clown teddie danced into the den. Since then, the plush line has expanded to 52 pieces, the majority of which are cuddly beanbag critters.

① N/A
New!

Ava (1999 Avon Exclusive)
Issued: 1999
To Be Closed: 1999
Original Price: $6.99
Value: $6.99

② #644366
New!
PHOTO UNAVAILABLE

Baby Plush (boy)
Issued: 1999 • Current
Original Price: $15
Value: $15

③ #644366
New!
PHOTO UNAVAILABLE

Baby Plush (girl)
Issued: 1999 • Current
Original Price: $15
Value: $15

④ #541222
New!

Bear w/Red Heart (1999 Event Exclusive)
Issued: 1999
To Be Closed: 1999
Original Price: $7
Value: $7

⑤ #549967
New!

Blue Bear With Ribbon (LE-48,000)
Issued: 1999
To Be Closed: 1999
Original Price: $25
Value: $25

PLUSH		
	Price Paid	Value Of My Collection
1.		
2.		
3.		
4.		
5.		
6.		
7.		
8.		
9.		
10.		
11.		
PENCIL TOTALS		

⑥ #654787

Christmas Bear
♪ *Have Yourself A Merry Little Christmas*
Issued: 1994
Out Of Production: 1995
Original Price: $55
Value: N/E

⑦ #111414

Clown Bear
♪ *Can't Smile Without You*
Issued: 1995
Out Of Production: 1996
Original Price: $40
Value: N/E

⑧ #914975

Elsa
We'll Always Be Special Friends
Issued: 1993
Out Of Production: 1996
Original Price: $50
Value: N/E

⑨ #914983

Elsa
I'll Always Be Here For You
Issued: 1993
Out Of Production: 1996
Original Price: $25
Value: N/E

⑩ #914991

Elsa
I'll Always Be Here For You
Issued: 1993
Out Of Production: 1996
Original Price: $15
Value: N/E

⑪ #644323
New!

Girl With Christmas Ribbon
Issued: 1999 • Current
Original Price: $15
Value: $15

① #644323 New!  **Girl With Christmas Ribbon** Issued: 1999 • Current Original Price: $15 Value: $15	**②** #644323 New!  **Girl With Christmas Ribbon** Issued: 1999 • Current Original Price: $15 Value: $15	**③** #631736 New!  **Jackie** Issued: 1999 • Current Original Price: $25 Value: $25	**④** #649155 New!  PHOTO UNAVAILABLE **Jennifer (LE-1999)** Issued: 1999 To Be Closed: 1999 Original Price: $25 Value: $25
⑤ #649155 New! PHOTO UNAVAILABLE **John (LE-1999)** Issued: 1999 To Be Closed: 1999 Original Price: $25 Value: $25	**⑥** #631736 New! **Karen** Issued: 1999 • Current Original Price: $25 Value: $25	**⑦** #916692  **Norman** *We'll Always Be Special Friends* Issued: 1993 Out Of Production: 1996 Original Price: $65 Value: N/E	**⑧** #916706  **Norman** *We'll Always Be Special Friends* Issued: 1993 Out Of Production: 1996 Original Price: $45 Value: N/E
⑨ #916714  **Norman** *We'll Always Be Special Friends* Issued: 1993 Out Of Production: 1996 Original Price: $30 Value: N/E	**⑩** #916730  **Norman** *We'll Always Be Special Friends* ♪ *Teddy Bear Picnic* Issued: 1993 Out Of Production: 1996 Original Price: $60 Value: N/E	**⑪** #639206 New!  **Rodney (Gift-To-Go Exclusive, sold as set, #646504, w/figurine)** Issued: 1999 To Be Closed: 1999 Original Price: $25 Value: $25	

PLUSH

	Price Paid	Value Of My Collection
1.		
2.		
3.		
4.		
5.		
6.		
7.		
8.		
9.		
10.		
11.		
12.		
13.		

HOLIDAY OCCASIONS PLUSH

14.		

PENCIL TOTALS

⑫ #610585 New!  **Santa With Hat (Event Exclusive)** Issued: 1999 To Be Retired: 1999 Original Price: $7 Value: $7	**⑬** #631736 New!  **Sara** Issued: 1999 • Current Original Price: $25 Value: $25	**⑭** #637998 New! PHOTO UNAVAILABLE **4th Of July** Issued: 1999 • Current Original Price: $7 Value: $7

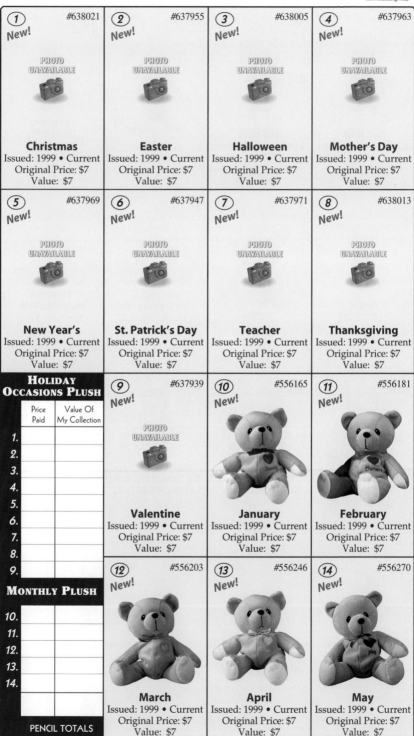

① #638021
New!

PHOTO UNAVAILABLE

Christmas
Issued: 1999 • Current
Original Price: $7
Value: $7

② #637955
New!

PHOTO UNAVAILABLE

Easter
Issued: 1999 • Current
Original Price: $7
Value: $7

③ #638005
New!

PHOTO UNAVAILABLE

Halloween
Issued: 1999 • Current
Original Price: $7
Value: $7

④ #637963
New!

PHOTO UNAVAILABLE

Mother's Day
Issued: 1999 • Current
Original Price: $7
Value: $7

⑤ #637969
New!

PHOTO UNAVAILABLE

New Year's
Issued: 1999 • Current
Original Price: $7
Value: $7

⑥ #637947
New!

PHOTO UNAVAILABLE

St. Patrick's Day
Issued: 1999 • Current
Original Price: $7
Value: $7

⑦ #637971
New!

PHOTO UNAVAILABLE

Teacher
Issued: 1999 • Current
Original Price: $7
Value: $7

⑧ #638013
New!

PHOTO UNAVAILABLE

Thanksgiving
Issued: 1999 • Current
Original Price: $7
Value: $7

⑨ #637939
New!

PHOTO UNAVAILABLE

Valentine
Issued: 1999 • Current
Original Price: $7
Value: $7

⑩ #556165
New!

January
Issued: 1999 • Current
Original Price: $7
Value: $7

⑪ #556181
New!

February
Issued: 1999 • Current
Original Price: $7
Value: $7

⑫ #556203
New!

March
Issued: 1999 • Current
Original Price: $7
Value: $7

⑬ #556246
New!

April
Issued: 1999 • Current
Original Price: $7
Value: $7

⑭ #556270
New!

May
Issued: 1999 • Current
Original Price: $7
Value: $7

HOLIDAY OCCASIONS PLUSH

	Price Paid	Value Of My Collection
1.		
2.		
3.		
4.		
5.		
6.		
7.		
8.		
9.		

MONTHLY PLUSH

10.		
11.		
12.		
13.		
14.		

PENCIL TOTALS

① #556289 — New!
June
Issued: 1999 • Current
Original Price: $7
Value: $7

② #556327 — New!
July
Issued: 1999 • Current
Original Price: $7
Value: $7

③ #556483 — New!
August
Issued: 1999 • Current
Original Price: $7
Value: $7

④ #556688 — New!
September
Issued: 1999 • Current
Original Price: $7
Value: $7

⑤ #556750 — New!
October
Issued: 1999 • Current
Original Price: $7
Value: $7

⑥ #556785 — New!
November
Issued: 1999 • Current
Original Price: $7
Value: $7

⑦ #556793 — New!
December
Issued: 1999 • Current
Original Price: $7
Value: $7

⑧ #505374 — New!
Best Friends
Issued: 1999 • Current
Original Price: $7
Value: $7

⑨ #505358 — New!
Hug Me
Issued: 1999 • Current
Original Price: $7
Value: $7

⑩ #505390 — New!
I Need You
Issued: 1999 • Current
Original Price: $7
Value: $7

⑪ #505331 — New!
Love Me
Issued: 1999 • Current
Original Price: $7
Value: $7

⑫ #505323 — New!
Miss You
Issued: 1999 • Current
Original Price: $7
Value: $7

⑬ #505382 — New!
Smile
Issued: 1999 • Current
Original Price: $7
Value: $7

MONTHLY PLUSH

	Price Paid	Value Of My Collection
1.		
2.		
3.		
4.		
5.		
6.		
7.		

T-SHIRT TEDDIES

8.		
9.		
10.		
11.		
12.		
13.		

PENCIL TOTALS

PLUSH

153

CHERISHED TEDDIES CLUB

Since the *Cherished Teddies Club* was established in 1995, membears have received Membearship figurines, pins, easel displays and other accessories. They also receive the yearly **Cherished Teddies** catalog, a subscription to *The Town Tattler*, a personalized membearship card and the opportunity to purchase exclusive Membears Only pieces.

1999

1999 COLLECTOR'S CLUB

	Price Paid	Value Of My Collection
1.		
2.		
3.		
4.		
5.		
6.		
PENCIL TOTALS		

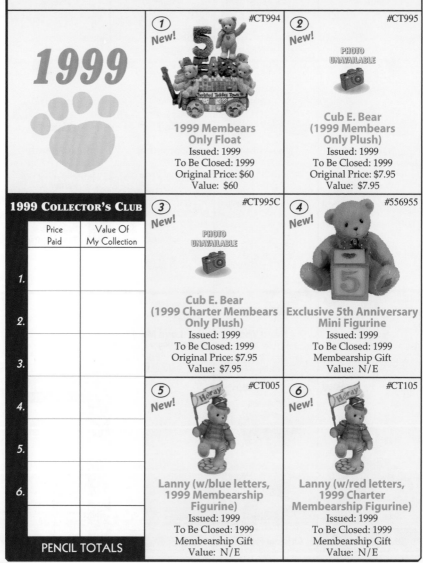

① New! #CT994
1999 Membears Only Float
Issued: 1999
To Be Closed: 1999
Original Price: $60
Value: $60

② New! #CT995
PHOTO UNAVAILABLE
Cub E. Bear (1999 Membears Only Plush)
Issued: 1999
To Be Closed: 1999
Original Price: $7.95
Value: $7.95

③ New! #CT995C
PHOTO UNAVAILABLE
Cub E. Bear (1999 Charter Membears Only Plush)
Issued: 1999
To Be Closed: 1999
Original Price: $7.95
Value: $7.95

④ New! #556955
Exclusive 5th Anniversary Mini Figurine
Issued: 1999
To Be Closed: 1999
Membership Gift
Value: N/E

⑤ New! #CT005
Lanny (w/blue letters, 1999 Membearship Figurine)
Issued: 1999
To Be Closed: 1999
Membership Gift
Value: N/E

⑥ New! #CT105
Lanny (w/red letters, 1999 Charter Membearship Figurine)
Issued: 1999
To Be Closed: 1999
Membership Gift
Value: N/E

① #CT993
New!

**Letty
(1999 Membearship
Figurine)**
Issued: 1999
To Be Closed: 1999
Original Price: $22.50
Value: $22.50

② #556947
New!

**Mini Clown Bear
(Early Renewal Gift,
designed to fit in
Letty's wagon)**
Issued: 1999
To Be Closed: 1999
Early Renewal Gift
Value: N/E

③ #631345
New!

**Ray (1999 Customer
Appreciation Figurine)**
Special Treats Make Life Complete
Issued: 1999
To Be Closed: 1999
Membearship Gift
Value: N/E

④ #CT205
New!

**Sculpted Lapel Pin (silver
tone, 1999 Lapel Pin)**
Issued: 1999
To Be Closed: 1999
Membership Gift
Value: N/E

⑤ #CT305
New!

**Sculpted Lapel Pin
(gold tone, 1999 Charter
Lapel Pin)**
Issued: 1999
To Be Closed: 1999
Membearship Gift
Value: N/E

⑥ #CT992
New!

**Vivienne
(1999 Membears
Only Figurine)**
Issued: 1999
To Be Closed: 1999
Original Price: $17.50
Value: $17.50

⑦ #CT991
New!

**Walter (1999 Membears
Only Figurine)**
Issued: 1999
To Be Closed: 1999
Original Price: $17.50
Value: $17.50

1998

⑧ #CRT442

**Cherished Teddies Club
"Bear Tag" Necklace**
Issued: 1998 • Closed: 1998
Membership Gift
Value: N/E

⑨ #CT983

**Cherished Teddies Town
Accessory Set (set/3, 1998
Membears Only Set)**
Issued: 1998 • Closed: 1998
Original Price: $17.50
Value: $17.50

1999 COLLECTOR'S CLUB

	Price Paid	Value Of My Collection
1.		
2.		
3.		
4.		
5.		
6.		
7.		

1998 COLLECTOR'S CLUB

8.		
9.		
PENCIL TOTALS		

COLLECTOR'S CLUB

① #CRT466

Cherished Teddies Town
**Teddie Care Center/
Ambulance Easel
Display (set/2)**
Issued: 1998 • Closed: 1998
Membearship Gift
Value: N/E

② #CT004

**Dr. Darlene Makebetter
(w/orange bag, 1998
Membearship Figurine)**
Issued: 1998 • Closed: 1998
Membearship Gift
Value: N/E

③ #CT104

**Dr. Darlene Makebetter
(w/pink bag, 1998 Charter
Membearship Figurine)**
Issued: 1998 • Closed: 1998
Membearship Gift
Value: N/E

④ #CT981

**Lela Nightingale (1998
Membears Only Figurine)**
Issued: 1998 • Closed: 1998
Original Price: $15
Value: $25

⑤ #CT982

**Wade Weathersbee (1998
Membears Only Figurine)**
Issued: 1998 • Closed: 1998
Original Price: $13.50
Value: $23

1997

	Price Paid	Value Of My Collection
1998 COLLECTOR'S CLUB		
1.		
2.		
3.		
4.		
5.		
1997 COLLECTOR'S CLUB		
6.		
7.		
8.		
9.		
PENCIL TOTALS		

⑥ #273554

**Amelia
(Cherished Rewards
Level #2)**
Issued: 1997 • Closed: 1998
Original Price: N/A
Value: N/E

⑦ #273198

**Benny
(Cherished Rewards,
Level #1)**
Issued: 1997 • Closed: 1998
Original Price: N/A
Value: N/E

⑧ #CT972

**Bernard and Bernice
Beary (1997 Membears
Only Figurine)**
Issued: 1997 • Closed: 1997
Original Price: $17.50
Value: $35

⑨ #297550

**Blaire Beary (Gift Club
Membearship Piece)**
Issued: 1997 • Closed: 1997
Membearship Gift
Value: $38

① #CRT279  **Cherished Teddies Club Membearship Pin** Issued: 1997 • Closed: 1997 Membearship Gift Value: $10	② #CRT289  **Cherished Teddies Town Depot Easel** Issued: 1997 • Closed: 1997 Membearship Gift Value: $10	③ #CT971  **Eleanor P. Beary (1997 Membears Only Figurine)** Issued: 1997 • Closed: 1997 Original Price: $17.50 Value: $34
④ #CT003  **Lloyd (w/red suitcase, 1997 Membears Only Figurine)** Issued: 1997 • Closed: 1997 Membearship Gift Value: $32	⑤ #CT103  **Lloyd (w/green suitcase, 1997 Charter Membears Only Figurine)** Issued: 1997 • Closed: 1997 Membearship Gift Value: $42	⑥ #277002  **Mary Jane (Cherished Rewards, Level #3)** Issued: 1997 • Closed: 1998 Original Price: N/A Value: N/E

1996

⑦ #CRT124

Cherished Teddies Club Membearship Pin
Issued: 1996 • Closed: 1996
Membearship Gift
Value: $14

⑧ #CT962

Emily E. Claire (1996 Membears Only Figurine)
Issued: 1996 • Closed: 1996
Original Price: $17.50
Value: $44

⑨ #CRT122

Hartford Printing Co., Firehouse #1 And The Honey Buns Shop Backdrop
Issued: 1996 • Closed: 1996
Membearship Gift
Value: $10

1997 COLLECTOR'S CLUB

	Price Paid	Value Of My Collection
1.		
2.		
3.		
4.		
5.		
6.		

1996 COLLECTOR'S CLUB

7.		
8.		
9.		

PENCIL TOTALS

COLLECTOR'S CLUB

(1) #CT002

**R. Harrison Hartford
(w/yellow pencil, 1996
Membearship Figurine)**
Issued: 1996 • Closed: 1996
Membearship Gift
Value: $42

(2) #CT102

**R. Harrison Hartford
(w/red pencil, 1996
Charter Membearship
Figurine)**
Issued: 1996 • Closed: 1996
Membearship Gift
Value: $63

(3) #CT961

**Kurtis D. Claw
(1996 Membears
Only Figurine)**
Issued: 1996 • Closed: 1996
Original Price: $17.50
Value: $54

(4) #CT953

***Town Tattler* Night Light
(1996 Membears
Only Figurine)**
Issued: 1996 • Closed: 1996
Original Price: $50
Value: $90

1995

(5) #CRT064

**Cherished Teddies Town
Backdrop**
Issued: 1995 • Closed: 1995
Membership Gift
Value: $16

1996 COLLECTOR'S CLUB

	Price Paid	Value Of My Collection
1.		
2.		
3.		
4.		

1995 COLLECTOR'S CLUB

5.		
6.		
7.		
8.		
9.		

PENCIL TOTALS

(6) #CT001

**Cub E. Bear
(1995 Membearship
Figurine)**
Issued: 1995 • Closed: 1995
Membearship Gift
Value: $62

(7) #CT952

**Hilary Hugabear (1995
Membears Only Figurine)**
Issued: 1995 • Closed: 1995
Original Price: $17.50
Value: $90

(8) #CRT065

**Key To *Cherished Teddies
Town* (pin)**
Issued: 1995 • Closed: 1995
Membership Gift
Value: $17

(9) #CT951

**Mayor Wilson T. Beary
(1995 Membears
Only Figurine)**
Issued: 1995 • Closed: 1995
Original Price: $20
Value: $84

Use these pages to record future **Cherished Teddies** *releases.*

CHERISHED TEDDIES	Original Price	Status	Year Mark	Market Value	Price Paid	Value Of My Collection
				PENCIL TOTALS		

*Use these pages to record future **Cherished Teddies** releases.*

CHERISHED TEDDIES	Original Price	Status	Year Mark	Market Value	Price Paid	Value Of My Collection
PENCIL TOTALS						

TOTAL VALUE OF MY COLLECTION

Record the value of your collection here by adding the pencil totals from the bottom of each Value Guide page.

CHERISHED TEDDIES			CHERISHED TEDDIES		
Page Number	Price Paid	Market Value	Page Number	Price Paid	Market Value
Page 37	17.50	53.0	Page 71		
Page 38	17.50	52.00	Page 72		
Page 39			Page 73		
Page 40	15.00	200.00	Page 74	30.00	58.00
Page 41	18.50	42.00	Page 75		
Page 42	18.50	44.00	Page 76		
Page 43			Page 77		
Page 44			Page 78		
Page 45			Page 79		
Page 46			Page 80		
Page 47	62.50	109.00	Page 81		
Page 48			Page 82		
Page 49			Page 83		
Page 50			Page 84		
Page 51			Page 85		
Page 52			Page 86		
Page 53			Page 87		
Page 54			Page 88		
Page 55	10.00	46.00	Page 89		
Page 56			Page 90		
Page 57	35.00	53.00	Page 91	17.50	42.00
Page 58			Page 92	53.50	133.00
Page 59			Page 93	25.00	42.00
Page 60	35.00	35.00	Page 94		
Page 61			Page 95		
Page 62	15.00	112.00	Page 96		
Page 63			Page 97	15.00	23.00
Page 64	17.50	45.00	Page 98		
Page 65	22.50	30.00	Page 99		
Page 66			Page 100		
Page 67	45.00	55.00	Page 101		
Page 68			Page 102		
Page 69			Page 103		
Page 70	15.00	45.00	Page 104		
TOTAL	327.00	868.00	**TOTAL**	141.00	298.00

TOTAL VALUE OF MY COLLECTION

Record the value of your collection here by adding the pencil totals from the bottom of each Value Guide page.

CHERISHED TEDDIES			CHERISHED TEDDIES		
Page Number	Price Paid	Market Value	Page Number	Price Paid	Market Value
Page 105			Page 133		
Page 106			Page 134		
Page 107			Page 135		
Page 108			Page 136		
Page 109	50.00	50.00	Page 137		
Page 110			Page 138		
Page 111	9.00	28.00	Page 139		
Page 112			Page 140		
Page 113			Page 141		
Page 114	62.50	151.00	Page 142		
Page 115	42.50	99.00	Page 143		
Page 116			Page 144		
Page 117			Page 145		
Page 118			Page 146		
Page 119			Page 147		
Page 120			Page 148		
Page 121			Page 149		
Page 122			Page 150		
Page 123			Page 151		
Page 124			Page 152		
Page 125			Page 153		
Page 126			Page 154		
Page 127			Page 155		
Page 128			Page 156		
Page 129			Page 157		
Page 130			Page 158		
Page 131			Page 159		
Page 132			Page 160		
TOTAL	164.00	328.00	**TOTAL**		

	GRAND TOTALS	632.00	1494.00
		PRICE PAID	**MARKET VALUE**

MORE CHERISHED TEDDIES® PRODUCTS

$\mathscr{F}$or those who just can't "bear" to be without their **Cherished Teddies** friends, Enesco has released a number of additional resin products featuring the adorable teddies. From candle huggers to stocking stuffers, there is a **Cherished Teddies** accessory for every room in the house, as well as a number of fashion products sure to add the perfect touch to any outfit.

Following is a listing of the resin **Cherished Teddies** accessory items. Pieces which are out of production are marked with an "O/P," while new releases for 1999 are marked with an asterisk (*).

BEAR-ETTES
❏ Bears With Bows
  Hair Pins (O/P) 273600
❏ Brown Eyed
  Susan (O/P) 273570
❏ Girl With
  Bow/Heart (O/P) 273597
❏ Girl With Purple
  Ribbon (O/P) 273619
❏ Girls With Bows (O/P). 273562
❏ Rose (O/P) 273589

BOOKMARKS
❏ *School Days*
  Bookmark 477346*

CANDLE HUGGERS
❏ Elf Candle Huggers
  (set/2, O/P) 651419

CONTAINERS
❏ Baby With Diaper
  (covered box) 203734
❏ Baby's 1st
  Christmas Bank 533319*

CONTAINERS, cont.
❏ Baby's 1st Christmas
  Covered Box 536903*
❏ Bears With Bows
  (vase, O/P) 203289
❏ Easter Basket (3 asst.) . 156523
❏ Gingerbear
  Glass Jars (with cork
  jar toppers, 3 asst.) 352640
❏ Halloween Treat Bags
  (3 asst., O/P) 141879
❏ Heart Shaped Cupid
  Covered Box 111015
❏ Heaven Has Blessed
  This Day (boy,
  Bible holder) 345105C
❏ Heaven Has Blessed
  This Day (girl,
  Bible holder) 309079C
❏ Heaven Has Blessed
  This Day (covered box
  with pendant) 303216
❏ Love Bears All Things
  (basket, O/P) 203246C
❏ Mini Flower Pots
  With Silk Flowers
  (3 asst.) 202983
❏ Mom – Maker Of
  Miracles (covered box
  with necklace) 306614
❏ Potpourri Holder 537667*
❏ Valentine Treat Bags
  (2 asst., O/P) 156582
❏ Wedding Covered Box
  (musical) 476897*

More Cherished Teddies® Products

ACROSS THE SEAS
(COVERED BOXES)

- [ ] American Boy 441155
- [ ] Australian Boy 441031
- [ ] Canadian Boy 441058
- [ ] Chinese Boy 441066
- [ ] Dutch Girl 441090
- [ ] English Boy 441139
- [ ] French Girl 441074
- [ ] German Boy 441082
- [ ] Italian Girl 441104
- [ ] Japanese Girl 441112
- [ ] Mexican Boy 441120
- [ ] Spanish Boy 441147

DRAWER PULLS

- [ ] Block Drawer Pull 203750
- [ ] Cherished Teddie
  Drawer Pull 279498

DISPLAYERS

- [ ] *Across The Seas*
  Display CRT234
- [ ] *Across The Seas*
  Wood Display 281506
- [ ] *Across The Seas*
  Wreath Display 470570
- [ ] *Antique Toy* Tool
  Bench Display 537640*
- [ ] *Beary-Go-Round*
  Carousel Display . . . 545007*
- [ ] *Beta Is For Bears*
  Easel Display 306312
- [ ] *Blossoms Of*
  Friendship Display . . CRT228
- [ ] *By the Sea,*
  By The Sea Display . . CRT233
- [ ] *Christmas Carol*
  Christmas Village
  Backdrop (O/P) CRT023
- [ ] *Count On Me* Display . . 302953
- [ ] *Down Strawberry*
  Lane Picket . . . .
  Fence Displayer CRT111

DISPLAYERS, cont.

- [ ] *Happily Ever After*
  Display 302589
- [ ] *Have A Cup Full Of*
  Sweetness Display . . . CRT335
- [ ] *Heart Of Gold* Basket
  Displayer 478954*
- [ ] *Holiday Dangling*
  Display (O/P) CRT227
- [ ] *Just Between Friends*
  Display 362956
- [ ] *Love Letters From*
  Teddie Display CRT230
- [ ] *Monthly Friends To*
  Cherish Shelf Talker . CRT089
- [ ] *Nursery Rhyme*
  Displayer (O/P). CRT013
- [ ] *Our Cherished Family*
  House Displayer CRT014
- [ ] *Our Cherished*
  Neighbearhood Fence
  Shelf Display 362697
- [ ] *Rainbow Lane*
  Displayer (O/P). CRT026
- [ ] *Santa's Workshop*
  Display CRT076
- [ ] *School Days*
  Basket/Backer
  Display 478997*

- [ ] *Sweetheart Ball*
  Displayer CRT096
- [ ] *T Is For Teddies*
  Display CRT101
- [ ] *T-Shirt Teddies*
  Basket Display 488585*
- [ ] *Teddie Triumphs*
  Shadow Box Display . 482072*
- [ ] *Through The Years*
  Display CRT004
- [ ] *Tis The Season* Window
  Pane Display (O/P) . . . CRT182

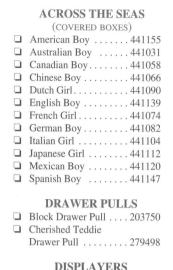

DISPLAYERS, cont.

- ❑ *Tis The Season* Wooden Mini Plate Rack Display (O/P) 213977
- ❑ Toy Shop Easel Backdrop (O/P). CRT002
- ❑ *We Bear Thanks* Backdrop (O/P) CRT083
- ❑ *Winter Bear Festival* Skating Pond Display . CRT334
- ❑ Wood Shadow Box Displayer 628557

LAMP SHADE TOPPERS

- ❑ Boy On Rocking Horse 135283
- ❑ Boy Sailor. 135283
- ❑ Girl With Bonnet 135283

LIGHT SWITCH COVERS

- ❑ Baby Light Switch Cover 203661

MAGNETS

- ❑ Boy Sailor (O/P). 902632
- ❑ Boy With Santa Cap (O/P) 951234
- ❑ Girl In Stocking (O/P) . 951234
- ❑ Girl Sailor (O/P). 902632

NECKLACES AND LOCKETS

- ❑ World's Greatest Mom Photo Heart Locket. 476994*
- ❑ Heart Of Gold (necklace). 477370*

PINS AND EARRINGS

- ❑ "An Angel To Watch Over You" (O/P) 176273
- ❑ "Boo-ti-ful" (O/P) 176230
- ❑ *Blossoms Of Friendship* (4 asst.). . . . 203033
  - ❑ *Brown Eyed Susan*
  - ❑ *Dahlia*
  - ❑ *Iris*
  - ❑ *Rose*
- ❑ Easter (O/P) 156574
- ❑ *Follow The Rainbow* . . 310425
- ❑ Halloween (O/P). 182958
- ❑ Heart Of Gold. 477362*
- ❑ Holiday (O/P). 141860
- ❑ "I Love You" Blocks (pin only, O/P) 203122
- ❑ Love (O/P) 156566
- ❑ "Love" Blocks (pin only, O/P) 203122
- ❑ Mom – Maker Of Miracles 303070
- ❑ St. Patrick's (O/P) 903132
- ❑ School Days 477060*
- ❑ Teddie With Block Lapel Pin (A-Z, sold separately, O/P) . . . 203297A-Z
- ❑ "XO" Blocks (pin only, O/P) 203122

STOCKING STUFFERS

- ❑ Stocking Stuffers (6 asst., O/P). 354058
  - ❑ *bookmark*
  - ❑ *holiday bear-ette*
  - ❑ *key chain*
  - ❑ *magnet*
  - ❑ *necklace*
  - ❑ *pin and earrings*

DISPLAY AND GIFT IDEAS

*T*he **Cherished Teddies** collection offers a wonderful selection of pieces that are sure to delight both the young and the young-at-heart. So, whether you're looking for a wonderful gift or a great display to accent any room in your home, you're sure to find it in Enesco's extraordinary line of lovable bears.

"BEAR" BACK RIDE

The *Beary-Go-Round Carousel*, a new series for 1999, is sure to inspire feelings of nostalgia. It doesn't matter where

or when you grew up – the image of a merry-go-round is probably in your memory. Why not relive those good times through a display? Surround your pieces with some dried hay or grass and add some brightly-colored silk flowers to the perimeter to invoke the feeling of a rural fairground. Set up a music box nearby to re-create the music coming from the calliope.

THE GREAT OUTDOORS

Pieces such as "Norm" and the characters from the *By The Sea, By The Sea* series look right at home in the great outdoors. While real water can get messy and may damage your pieces, the effect of water is easily recreated through some blue colored cellophane, which can be found in most supermarkets. Surround your pieces with some clean, dry grass and pebbles to complete the look. "Rose" looks adorable displayed in a miniature indoor garden surrounded by plastic flowers. To create an adorable pumpkin patch scene, place "Daniel" (with his pumpkin) and the "Halloween Mini Figurines" in a display with some healthy looking plant sprouts.

A BASKET FULL OF LOVE

A creative idea for Easter, birthdays, baby showers and the like is a themed gift basket. Garnish a basket (be creative with sizes and shapes) with some Easter grass. Then, fill the basket with a few **Cherished Teddies** pieces and other appropriate accessories. Some ideas include mixing "Brooke," or any of the pieces in the *Nursery Rhyme Series* with some diaper pins, bibs and bottles or including a few of the teddies in teacups in a "get-well" basket filled with herbal teas.

WINTER WONDERLAND

As the Christmas season rolls around, get in the spirit with some festive holiday displays. The pieces in *Santa Express, Santa Series* and *Old Fashioned Country Christmas* can be used to create a tiny North Pole village right in your own home. Some fluffy cottonballs create the look of a snow-covered landscape, while blinking Christmas lights can be set up to help your little "elves" see as they work into the night. Add some trees and rocks for a natural effect or fashion bridges, sidewalks and walls from sugar cubes or peppermint candy for a more whimsical touch. You can even try incorporating this display into a clear, hard-sided box fashioned with ribbons and bows for a great Christmas gift!

The most important thing to remember when creating displays or personalized gifts is to use your creativity and have fun!

*W*hile your collection may begin with **Cherished Teddies** pieces that catch your eye on your local store shelves, before long you may start to look for pieces that aren't so readily available and wonder where to find them. Whatever the reason your desired piece is not on that shelf – whether it was retired, taken out of production or only available for a limited time – chances are that with a little luck and a lot of patience, you'll have a successful hunt for those teddies on the secondary market.

What is the secondary market? Basically, it's the principles of supply and demand at work. When a piece is easily available, its price will most likely be close to, or that of, the original retail price. However, if the demand for a piece outweighs the number produced or the amount available through retailers diminishes, the value of the piece will more than likely rise. Limited editions, exclusives or pieces that are retired often become difficult to find and highly sought after, therefore creating secondary market activity.

GONE, BUT NOT FORGOTTEN

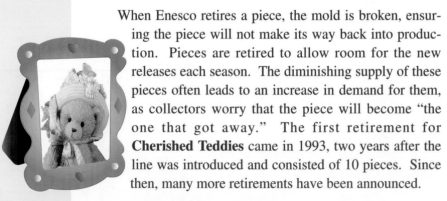

When Enesco retires a piece, the mold is broken, ensuring the piece will not make its way back into production. Pieces are retired to allow room for the new releases each season. The diminishing supply of these pieces often leads to an increase in demand for them, as collectors worry that the piece will become "the one that got away." The first retirement for **Cherished Teddies** came in 1993, two years after the line was introduced and consisted of 10 pieces. Since then, many more retirements have been announced.

WE SHALL RETURN . . . MAYBE

Sometimes, Enesco may choose to "suspend" a piece. Simply put, this means that while production is halted, the mold is kept intact. The suspension may be temporary and the pieces may return to stores at any given time. However, during a piece's suspension, availability is bound to run short, causing collectors to seek it on the secondary market at an increased price, despite the possibility that the piece could return to production at the regular retail price.

ONLY FOR A LIMITED TIME

Retail stores often hold **Cherished Teddies** events at which an exclusive piece is offered. Since the piece is available only for a very short period of time, the demand becomes high rather quickly, often causing a dramatic increase in value. Additionally, on occasion, specific retailers, such as Gift Creations Concepts stores, NALED stores or Avon, may have exclusive pieces available. Catalog exclusives and event pieces can be hard to track down, so it pays to keep informed on what's happening in the world of **Cherished Teddies** figurines. Other exclusive pieces include those available only to members of the *Cherished Teddies Club* and special pieces (usually slightly different versions of U.S. pieces) that are sold only in international markets.

In addition to exclusives, each year there are several limited editions available in the general line that are available

for a limited production time or quantity. **Cherished Teddies** Limited editions can either be limited to a specific time period ("LE-1996") or to a specific quantity produced ("LE-25,000"). Either way, this limited availability tends to cause the design to gain more value on the secondary market than that of a general release that is more readily available.

Remarkable!

Year marks began appearing on the bottoms of **Cherished Teddies** figurines in 1993 as a way for Enesco to keep track of when a piece was produced. Prior to this time, only a random letter appeared before the handwritten registration. The year mark consists of a digit that corresponds with the year a figurine was produced; so a "3" would mean that a piece was issued in 1993. It is important to note, however, that pieces released in the spring may have the previous year's mark, as it also reflects the year in which the piece was introduced to retailers. In recent years, collectors have started to assess value to pieces that have an earlier year mark, even if the design is still current.

A Perfect "10"

If you're selling a piece, it's very important to note its condition, as any damage or wear may decrease its value. Also note if the piece has been signed, comes with its original box or has the Certificate of Adoption (each **Cherished Teddies** figurine comes with one) as all of these factors will increase the market value. Communication is key and what you discover will ensure that you not only pay a fair price, but that you know what you're paying for.

Where Do I Go?

Finding the secondary market can be quite easy. As many people have access to the Internet, everything from chatting with other collectors to finding a piece for sale in electronic classifieds is literally at your fingertips.

There are many web sites that offer information about

the **Cherished Teddies** line. One of the best is the official Enesco site at www.enesco.com. Other alternative sites are available and by performing a search, you can find collectors and secondary market dealers with just a few clicks of a mouse. Auction sites have also become a popular place to locate hard-to-find pieces. One of the advantages of these sites is that most provide a history of the seller and the auctions they've been involved with. But remember, you can never be too careful when dealing with the Internet.

Another popular means of finding **Cherished Teddies** figurines is through exchanges. The exchange services acts as a liaison between the parties by publishing a list of pieces for sale, along with asking prices. Most exchanges are monthly publications that require a subscription and usually charge a 10 to 20 percent commission for each piece sold through their service.

Retailers normally do not take part in the secondary market, but some can provide direction to lead you to other sources. The newspaper classifieds are another means of approaching the secondary market. And an even more direct classified source can be found in collectible magazines.

No matter what the monetary value may be of your **Cherished Teddies** collection, it's important to remember why you began collecting them in the first place – because they're irresistible and sure to provide truly sentimental value.

Secondary Market Exchanges

Collectible Exchange, Inc.
6621 Columbiana Road
New Middletown, OH 44442
(800) 752-3208

Donna's Collectibles Exchange
703 Endeavor Drive South
Winter Springs, FL 32708
(800) 480-5105
www.donnascollexch.com

New England Collectibles Exchange
Bob Dorman
201 Pine Avenue
Clarksburg, MA 01247
(413) 663-3643
www.collectiblesbroker.com

VARIATIONS

VARIATIONS

A variation occurs when there's a difference between pieces of the same design. Changes in color, size, and shape, as well as simple misspellings, are all examples of variations. Even though **Cherished Teddies** designs are produced from the same molds, slight changes at any point during the production process can cause variations. Because much of the detailed work is done by hand, many of these variations are due to human error, even though Enesco adheres to strict production standards. Sometimes, however, a change in design can be deliberately made during production, oftentimes to fix a particular flaw or to change a specific color in a piece.

This section lists some of the most popular and acknowledged variations in the **Cherished Teddies** line, all of which have shown an increase in value on the secondary market.

Standard

Variation

Age 6 (#911283) . . . This adorable teddie first appeared in 1993 and has been spotted with a white patch with green dots on his right elbow.

Amy (#910732) . . . This little teddie wasn't happy with the color of bow she was wearing in her hair, so after a short time she changed it! When Amy was first introduced in 1993, her hair bow was lavender. The current version has a white bow.

Variation

Standard

Standard

Variation

Angel (ornament, #950777), Angel On Bell (bell, #906530), Angie (figurine, #951137) . . . The variation on all three of these pieces is the finish on the halo. On the earlier pieces, the halo is metal and is a gold

Standard

Variation

Variation

Standard

color with a shiny finish. Later the halo was made of resin and has a darker finish.

Beth and Blossom (#950564) . . . A production problem is the reason for the variation on this piece. When the duo first began arriving

in retail stores, there was a butterfly on the handle of the basket in which the bears are sitting. Shortly thereafter, new figurines were produced without the butterfly, as it was found to break loose during shipment.

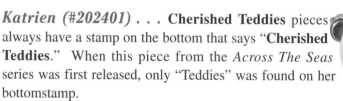

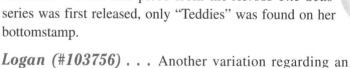

Standard

Variation

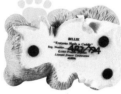

Variation

Billy (#624896) . . .
A misspelled word led to the variation of this little teddie. On some piece's the incorrect "Billie," was printed on the underside.

Katrien (#202401) . . . **Cherished Teddies** pieces always have a stamp on the bottom that says "**Cherished Teddies**." When this piece from the *Across The Seas* series was first released, only "Teddies" was found on her bottomstamp.

Variation

Logan (#103756) . . . Another variation regarding an understamp showed up on early versions of "Logan." This piece, part of the *Circus* series, was erroneously given limited edition status when the incorrect "Limited To Year Of Production" was stamped on the underside of the figurine.

Variation

VARIATIONS

Mark (#914770) . . . When this "March" figurine from the *Monthly Friends To Cherish* series was first released, the teddie's kite had a tail. However, the piece can be found without the tail as well.

Standard

Variation

Marie (#910767) . . . This figurine portrays Marie sitting on a blanket with a tea set. In one version, there's a big pink heart on the front of the teapot and Marie's napkin is white and lavender. The variation has a white heart on the teapot and a blue napkin.

Variation

Standard

Michael and Michelle (#910775) . . . While these two teddies were sleeping, someone changed the color of their pillow. The common version has a white ruffle around the pillow, but some pieces have been known to show up with a yellow ruffle.

Standard

Variation

Mother (#624861) . . . Although a mother's love never changes, the inspirational message on this piece has. In the United States, the figurine says "A Mother's Love Bears All Things," but on pieces sold in Canada and the U.K. "Mother's" was changed to "Mum('s)."

"A Mum Love Bears All Things"
Reg. 4ee3/280
© 1993 P.H. 624861

Variation

Pat (#141313) . . . The doll lying at the base of the "basket" in which this teddie sits experienced a change. The scarecrow companion was featured wearing a white and brown checked shirt in the standard version, while the variation sports a blue hue.

Patrice (#911429) . . . The little bunny in this figurine has been spotted with two different colored tails. On some of the pieces its tail is white, while on others, the tail is pink.

Standard

Variation

Peter (#104973) . . . The eggs "Peter" is delivering have been noted to differ through the years. When first released, the eggs in the basket were dark in color and the base of the figurine was thin. Now, the eggs are lighter and the piece has a thicker base.

Signage Plaque (#951005) . . . Three versions of this **Cherished Teddies** plaque exist with variations occurring on both the logo on the front of the plaque and the writing on the bottomstamp. The first version of the piece has "Hamilton Gifts Limited" beneath the name on the sign and "Lic. Hamilton Gifts" on the bottom. On the second release, the wording on the front changed to "By Enesco" and the bottom read "Lic. Hamilton Gifts." The third and final version of this piece still says "By Enesco" on the sign, but the bottomstamp now says "Lic. Enesco Corp."

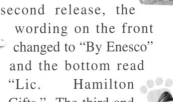

Hamilton Logo

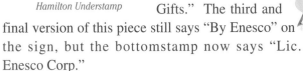

Hamilton Understamp

Enesco Logo

Enesco Understamp

Theadore, Samantha and Tyler (#950505) . . . The largest of these three teddies normally wears a square white patch on his right arm, but for a brief time, the arm patch was a blue heart.

VARIATIONS

Christy (#128023), Dorothy (#128023), Millie (#128023) . . . All three of these teddies changed their looks when they spiced up their wardrobes with brightly colored ribbons.

Standard

Variation

Standard

Variation

Standard

Variation

Jacki (#950432), Karen (#950432), Sara (#950432) . . . The standard version for all three of these bears include hair bows with polka-dots and a solid-colored heart on their chests. In alternate versions, the hair bows feature different designs, their hearts sport dots and patches appear on their arms.

Standard

Variation

Standard

Standard

Variation

Standard   *Variation*

ON THEIR WAY?

There are no rules that determine which errors or production changes will acquire top dollar value on the secondary market. Some, like those listed below, are recognized by collectors but do not command a higher value than the standard pieces.

Beth (#950637) . . . As "Beth" got older, she got bit taller as well. The first version of this sweet figurine is smaller than the version that was available before being retired in 1995.

Judy (#203491) . . . This teddie has been spotted taking shelter under two different umbrellas. While the standard version's umbrella is painted in pastel colors, the variation has primary colors that are much brighter.

Variation

Standard

Olga (#182966) . . . The fact that this was a limited edition piece wasn't the only thing that caught the eye of collectors. The curious squirrel standing beside the tree was spotted with different color fur.

Timothy (#910740) . . . The cat in this figurine defines the phrase, "finicky feline." While the color of his fur on most versions of the figurine was pink, sometimes he was seen wearing a white coat.

INSURING YOUR COLLECTION

*W*hen insuring your collection, there are three major points to consider:

KNOW YOUR COVERAGE — Collectibles are typically included in homeowner's or renter's insurance policies. Ask your agent if your policy covers fire, theft, floods, hurricanes, earthquakes and damage or breakage from routine handling. Also, ask if your policy covers claims at "current replacement value" – the amount it would cost to replace items if they were damaged, lost or stolen – which is extremely important since the secondary market value of some pieces may well exceed their original retail price.

DOCUMENT YOUR COLLECTION — In the event of a loss, you will need a record of the contents and value of your collection. Ask your insurance agent what information is acceptable. Keep receipts and an inventory of your collection in a different location, such as a safe deposit box. Include the purchase date, price paid, size, issue year, edition limit/number, special markings and secondary market value for each piece. Photographs and video footage with close-up views of each piece are good back-ups.

> Many companies will accept a reputable secondary market price guide – such as the Collector's Value Guide™ – as a valid source for determining your collection's value.

WEIGH THE RISK — To determine the coverage you need, calculate how much it would cost to replace your collection and compare it to the total amount your current policy would pay. To insure your collection for a specific dollar amount, ask your agent about adding a Personal Articles Floater or a Fine Arts Floater or "rider" to your policy, or insuring your collection under a totally separate policy. As with all insurance, you must weigh the risk of loss against the cost of additional coverage.

assorted — pieces that share the same stock number, but can be purchased separately.

bottomstamp — also called an "understamp," any identifying marks on the underside of a figurine.

catalog exclusive — pieces offered exclusively to groups of retailers who participate in selected gift catalog programs. These pieces may be released into the general line at a later time.

closed edition — a piece limited by time or quantity that is no longer available from the manufacturer.

collectible — anything and everything that is "able to be collected," such as figurines and dolls. Even *eight track tapes* can be considered a "collectible," but it is generally recognized that a true collectible should be something that increases in value over time.

current — a piece that is in current production and available in retail stores.

event piece — a piece specially made for sale only at a **Cherished Teddies** promotional event.

letter mark – for **Cherished Teddies** figurines produced from 1991 to 1992, this is the first character in the handwritten registration number.

limited edition (LE) — a piece scheduled for a predetermined production quantity or time.

out of production — a term used to note accessory items that are no longer available to retailers but are not officially "retired" or "suspended."

primary market — the conventional collectibles purchasing process in which collectors buy directly from dealers at issue price.

registration number — the handwritten number and letter combination that appears on the bottom of **Cherished Teddies** resin figurines.

retired — a piece that is taken out of production, never to be made again.

secondary market — the source for buying and selling collectibles according to basic supply-and-demand principles ("pay what the market will bear"). Popular pieces that are sold out or have been retired can appreciate in value above the original issue price.

suspended — a piece that has been removed from production by the manufacturer but may return in the future.

temporarily out of production (TOPS) — a term that changed to "suspended" in 1996.

variations — items that have color, design or printed text changes from the "original" piece, whether intentional or not. Some of these changes are minor, while some are important enough to affect the value of a piece on the secondary market.

year mark — for **Cherished Teddies** figurines produced from 1993 to 1999, this is the number that appears as the first character in the registration number, specifying the year the piece was produced (e.g., "3" for 1993).

– Key –

All **Cherished Teddies** resin pieces are listed below in numerical order by stock number. The first number refers to the piece's location within the Value Guide section and the second to the box in which it is pictured on that page. For additional pieces, please see the "More Cherished Teddies Products" section on pages 163-165.

NUMERICAL INDEX

Acknowledgements

CheckerBee Publishing would like to thank Michelle Davidson, Kristi Francis and all the Cherished Teddies retailers and collectors who contributed their valuable time to assist us with this book. Many thanks to the great people at Enesco.

– Key –

All Cherished Teddies resin pieces are listed below in alphabetical order. The first number refers to the piece's location within the Value Guide section and the second to the box in which it is pictured on that page. For additional pieces, see the "More Cherished Teddies Products" section on pages 163-165.

Alphabetical Index

ALPHABETICAL INDEX

ALPHABETICAL INDEX

ALPHABETICAL INDEX

189

ALPHABETICAL INDEX

ALPHABETICAL INDEX